JOHN MAYER LIVE
THE GREAT GUITAR PERFORMANCES

CONTENTS

Cover Photo by Tim Gurr

Transcribed by Jeff Jacobson
(Additional transcribing by Steve Gorenberg and Dave Celentano)

Cherry Lane Music Company
Director of Publications/Project Editor: Mark Phillips

ISBN 978-1-60378-242-5

Visit our website at www.cherrylaneprint.com

BELIEF

Words and Music by
John Mayer

*Chord symbols reflect overall harmony.

Verse

Gtr. 1: w/ Riff A (2 times)

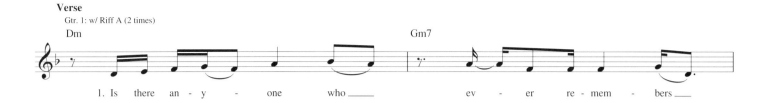

1. Is there an - y - one who _____ ev - er re - mem - bers _____

chang - ing their mind from _____ the paint on a sign?

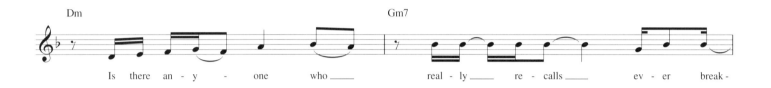

Is there an - y - one who _____ real - ly _____ re - calls _____ ev - er break -

- ing rank _____ at all _____ for some - thing some - one yelled _____ real loud _____ one _____ time?

Pre-Chorus

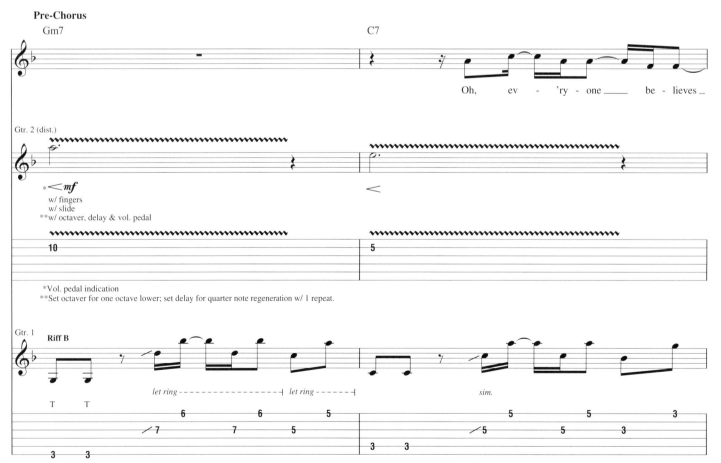

Oh, ev - 'ry - one _____ be - lieves _____

*Vol. pedal indication
**Set octaver for one octave lower; set delay for quarter note regeneration w/ 1 repeat.

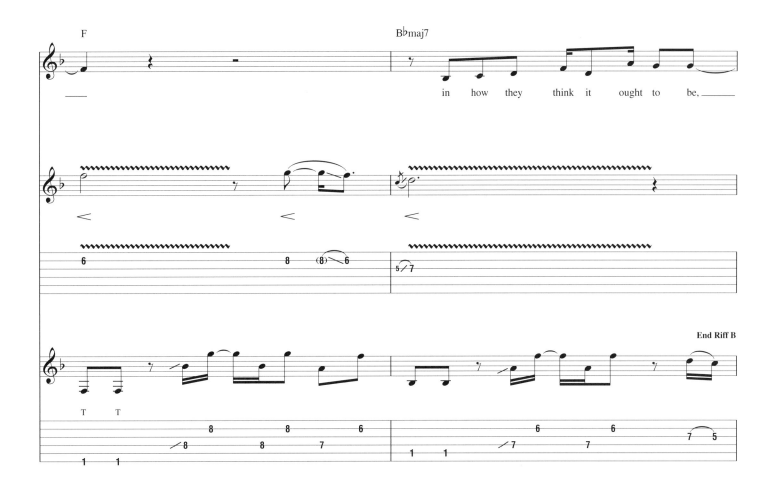

in how they think it ought to be, _____

End Riff B

__ yeah.

Oh, ev - 'ry - one ___ be - lieves, __

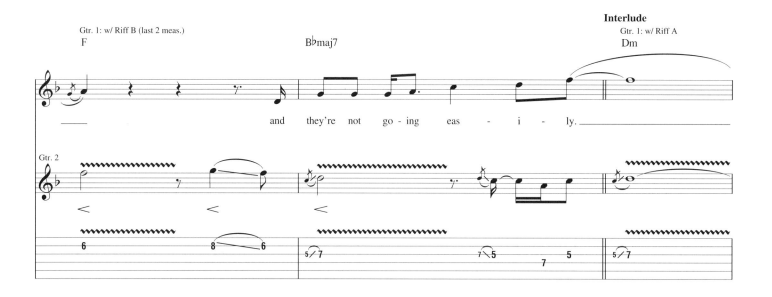

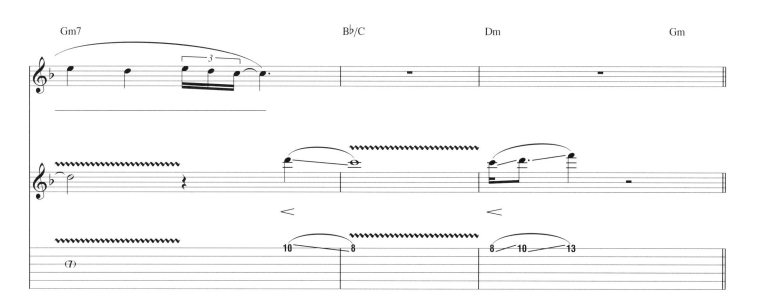

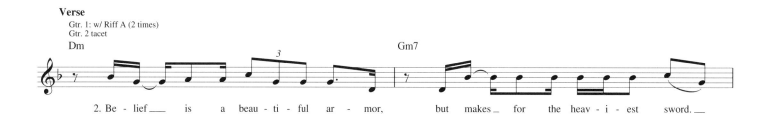

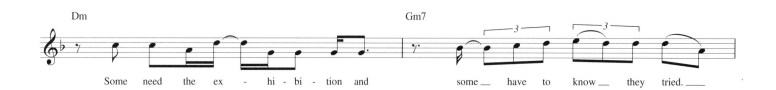

Pre-Chorus

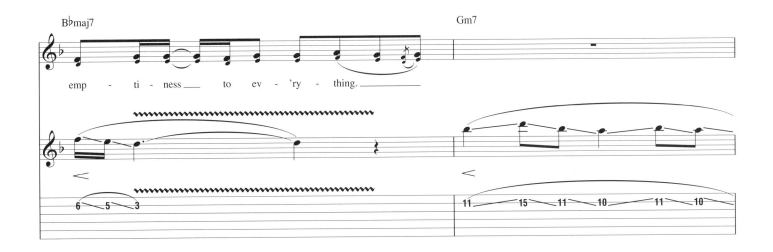

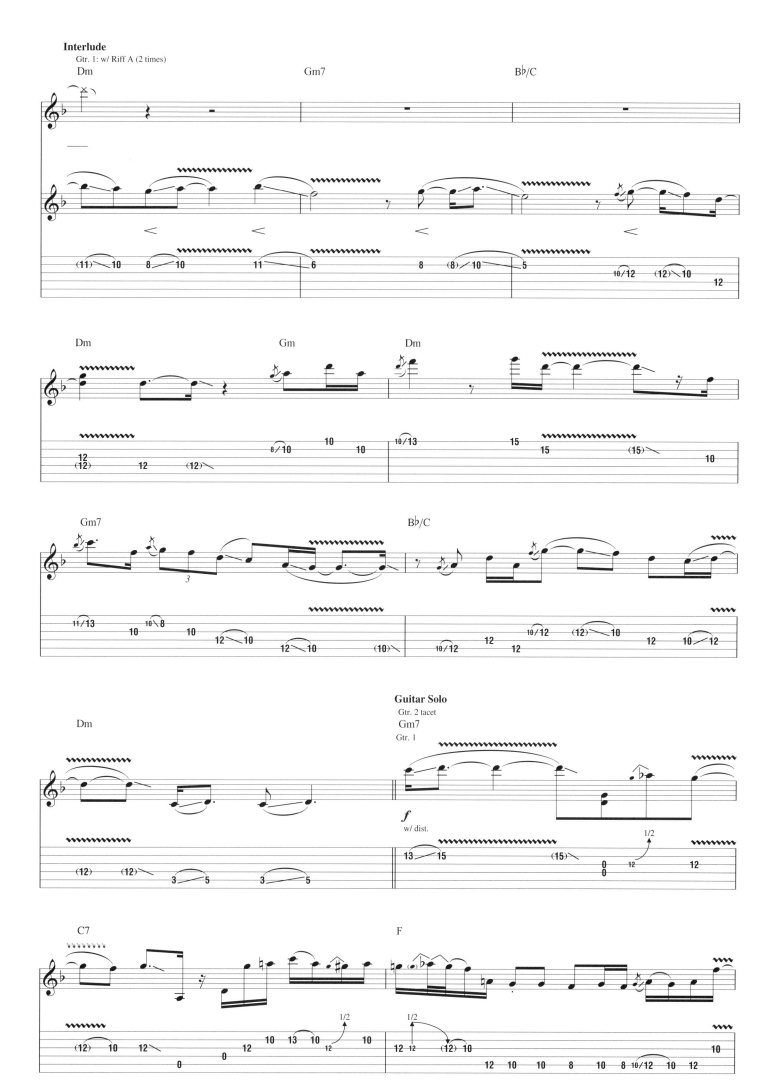

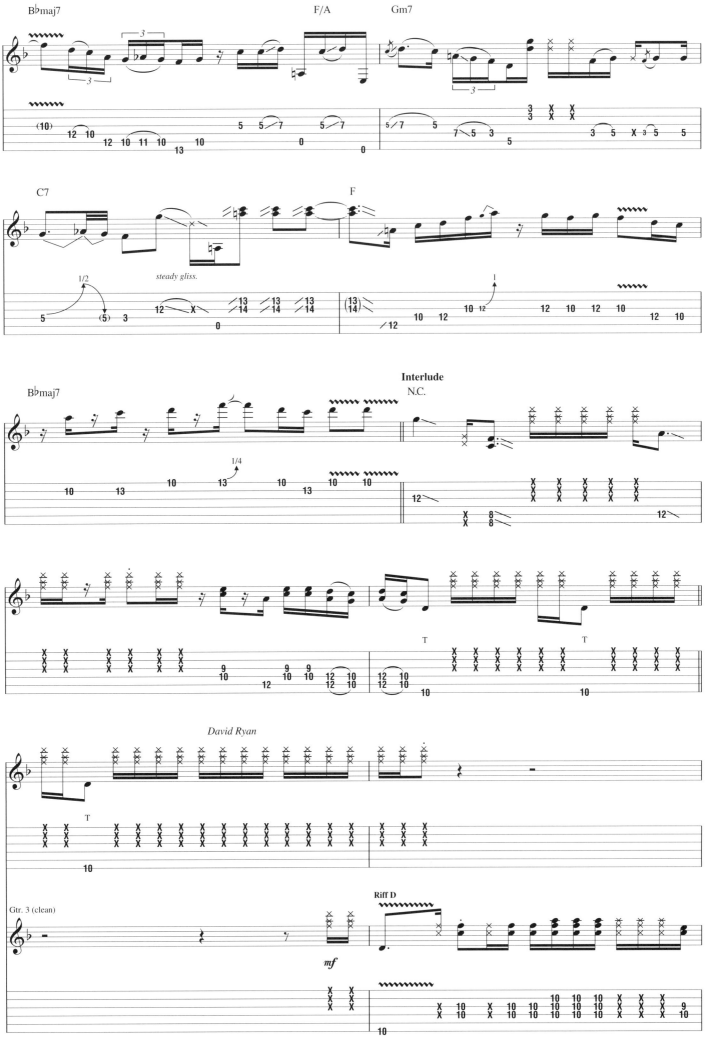

BLUES INTRO

Words and Music by
John Mayer

A

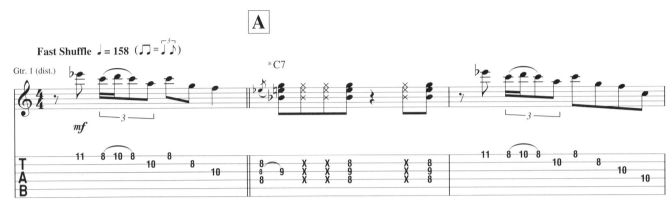

*Chord symbols reflect basic harmony.

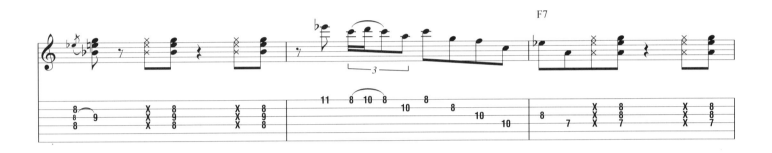

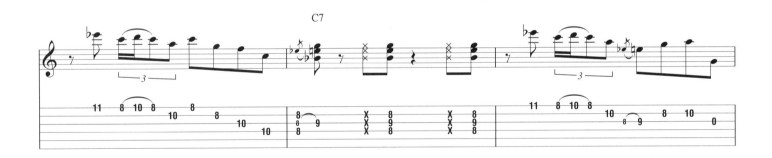

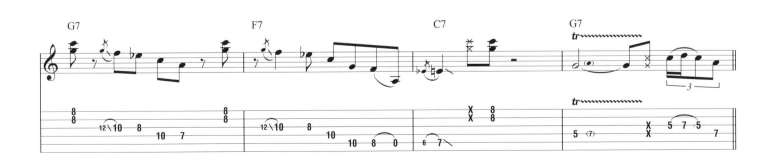

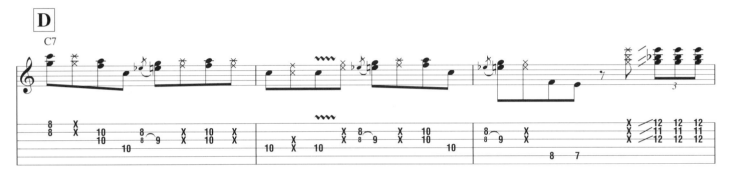

D

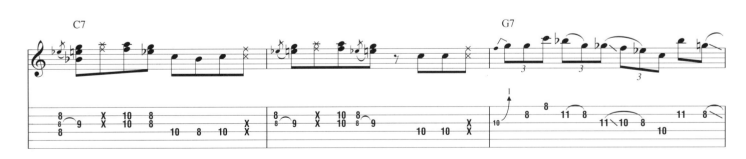

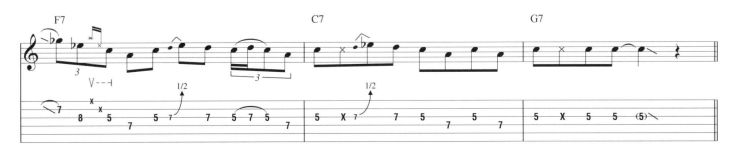

16

G

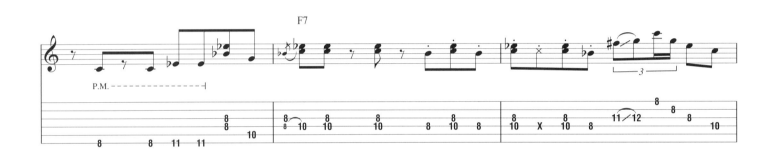

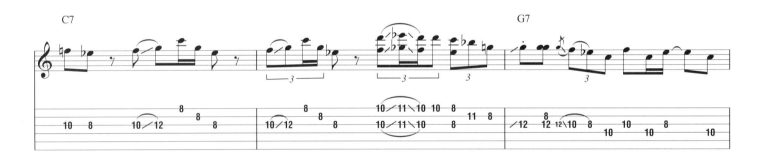

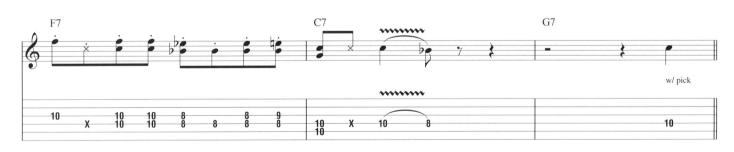

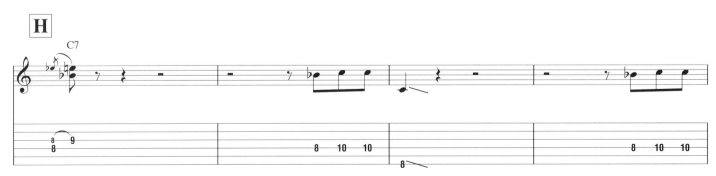

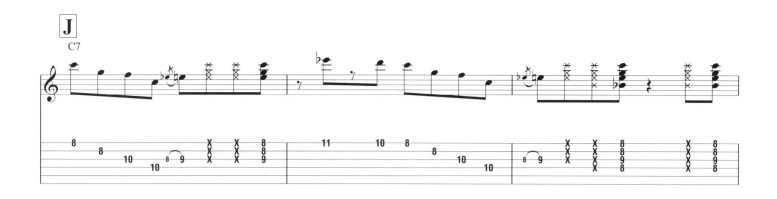

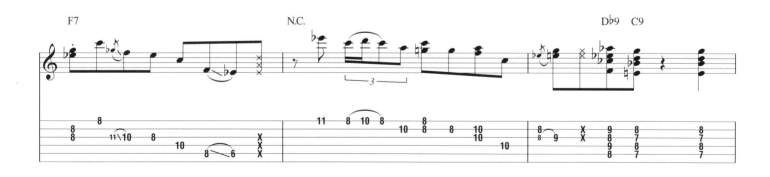

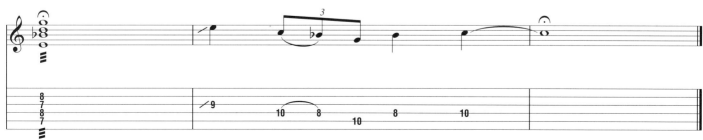

COME WHEN I CALL

Words and Music by
John Mayer

why won't you come when I call? ____

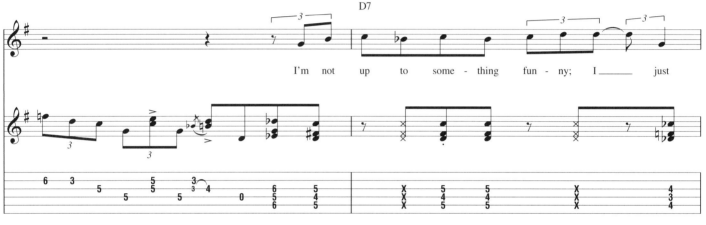

I'm not up to some - thing fun - ny; I ____ just

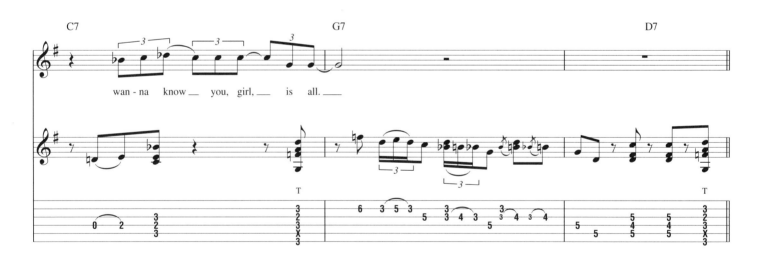

wan - na know __ you, girl, __ is all. __

Verse

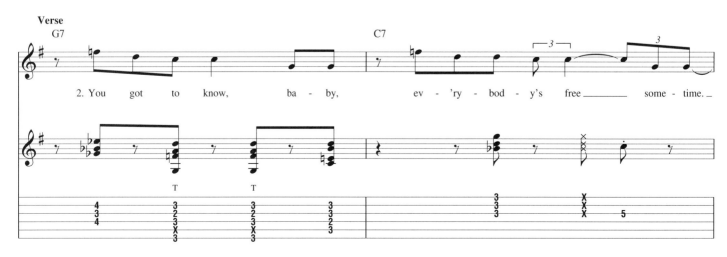

2. You got to know, ba - by, ev - 'ry - bod - y's free ____ some - time. __

Bridge

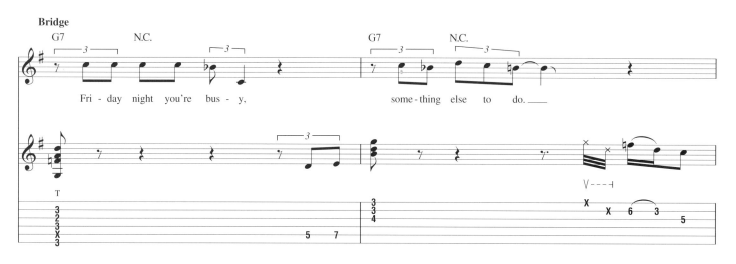

Fri - day night you're bus - y, some - thing else to do. ___

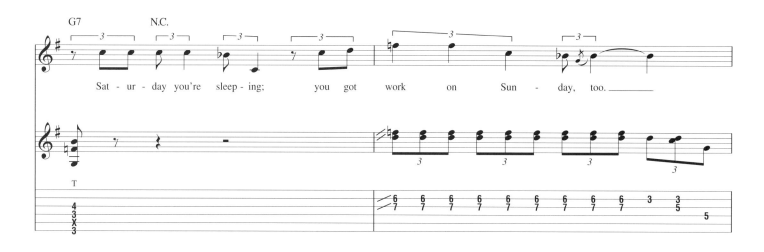

Sat - ur - day you're sleep - ing; you got work on Sun - day, too. ___

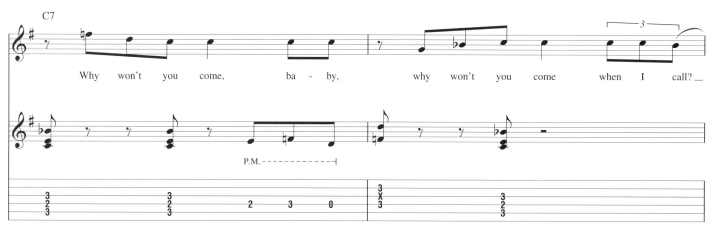

Why won't you come, ba - by, why won't you come when I call? ___

24

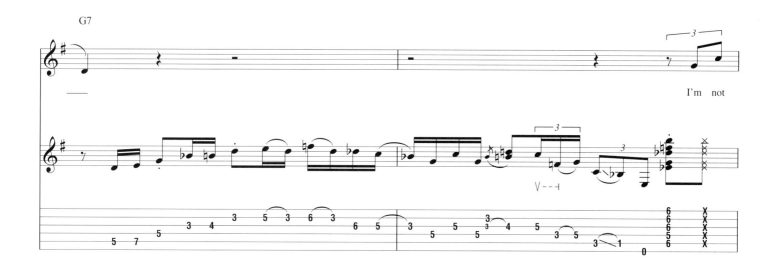

G7

I'm not

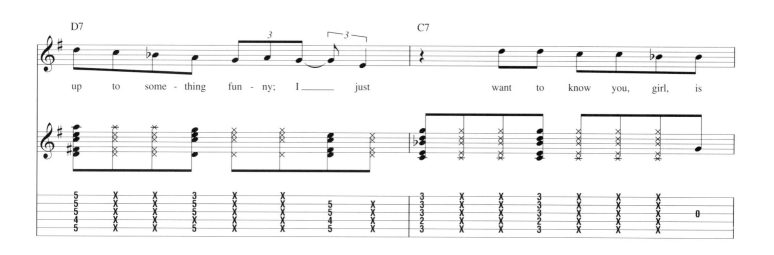

D7   C7

up   to   some - thing   fun - ny;   I _____ just   want   to   know   you,   girl,   is

G7

all.

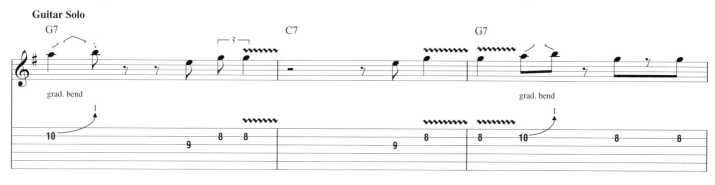

Guitar Solo

G7   C7   G7

grad. bend   grad. bend

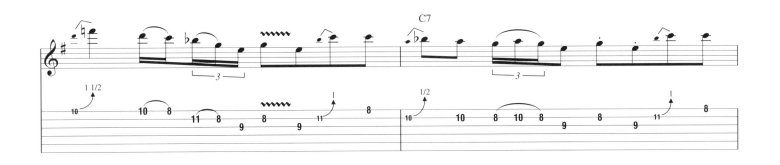

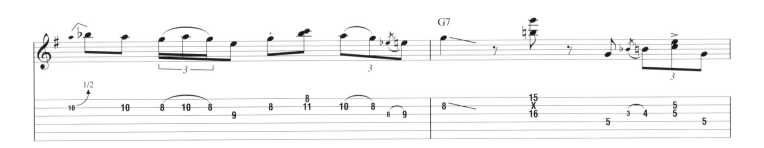

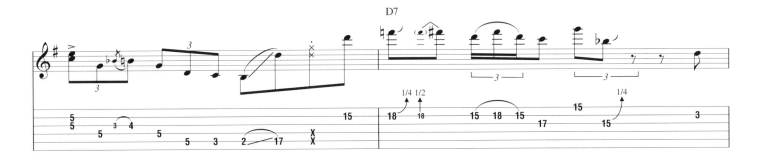

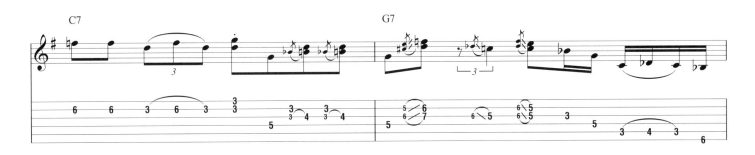

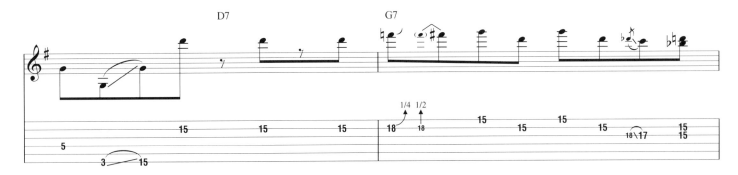

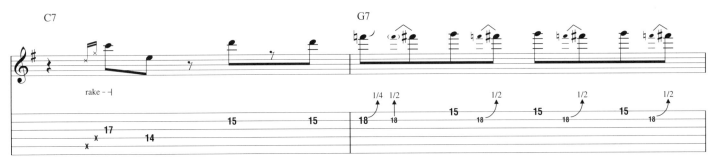

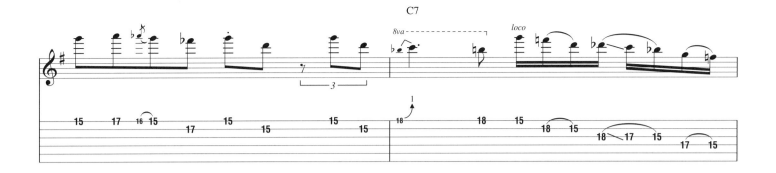

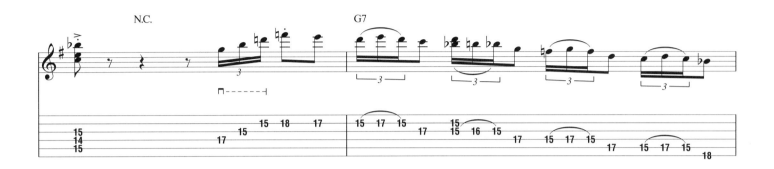

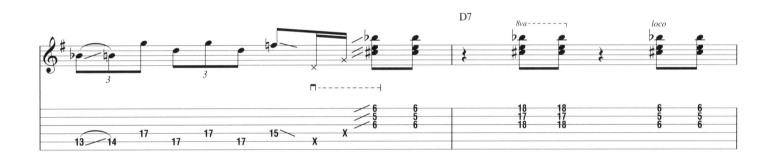

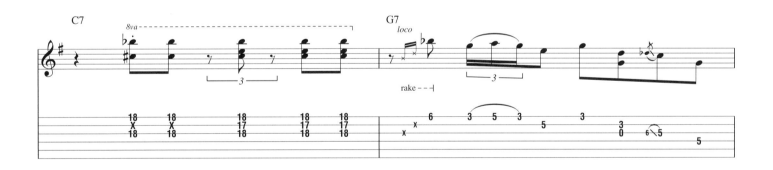

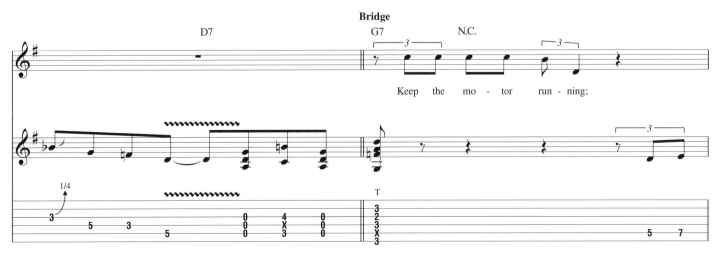

Keep the mo - tor run - ning;

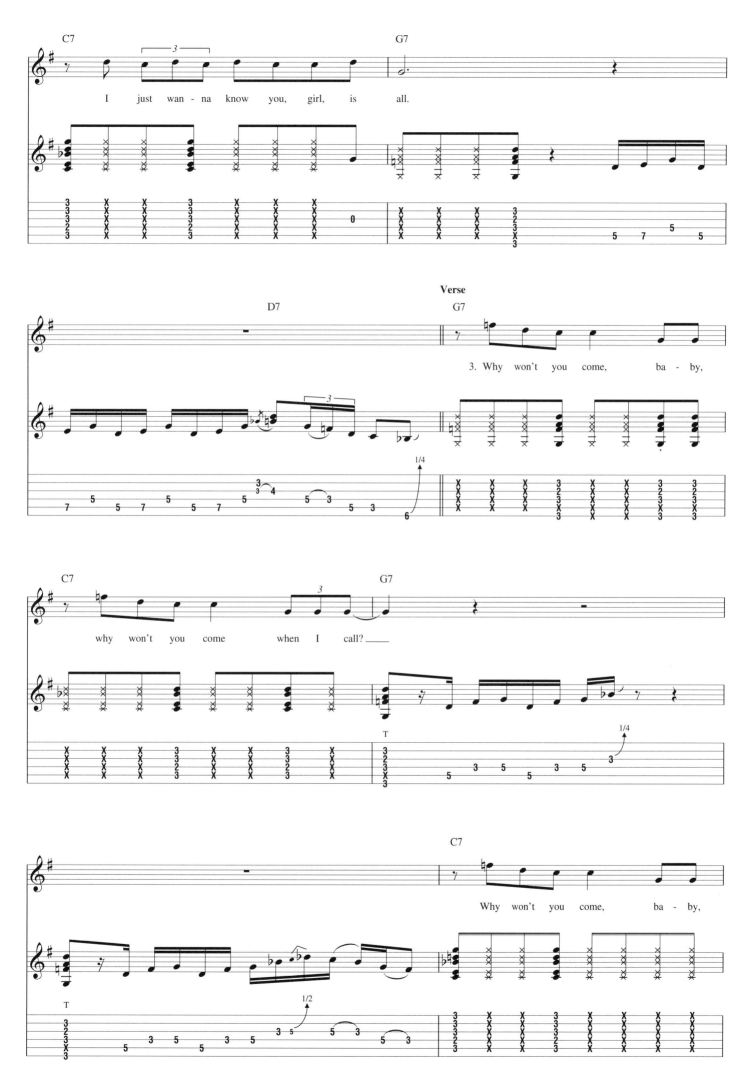

Verse

I just wan-na know you, girl, is all.

3. Why won't you come, ba - by,

why won't you come when I call? ____

Why won't you come, ba - by,

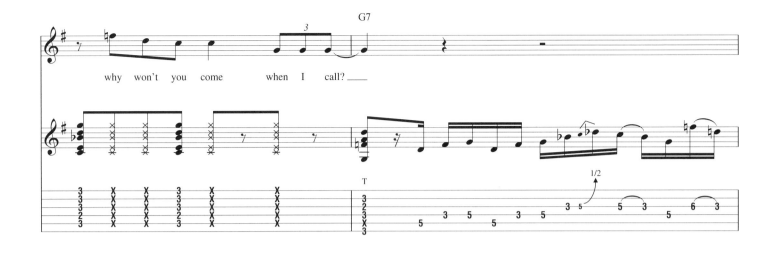

why won't you come when I call? ____

I'm not up to some-thing fun-ny; I____ just,

just wan - na know you, girl, is all.

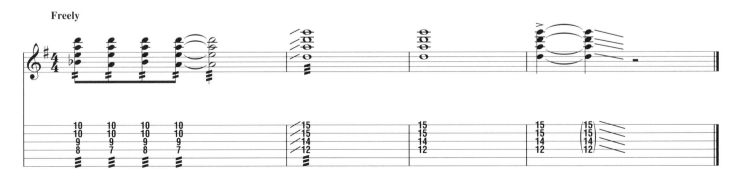

Freely

COMFORTABLE

Words and Music by
John Mayer and Clay Cook

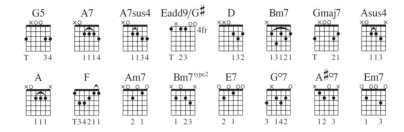

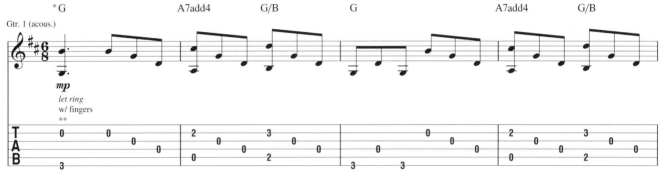

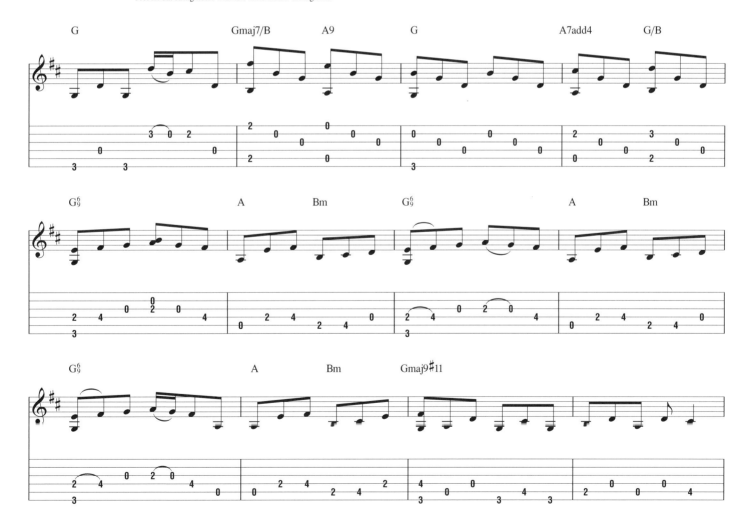

*All music sounds a minor 3rd higher than indicated due to capo. Capoed fret is "0" in tab.

**Fret all 6th string notes with left-hand thumb throughout.

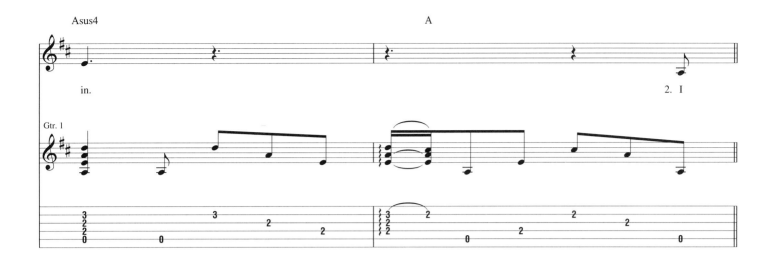

Verse

Gtr. 1: w/ Rhy. Fig. 1

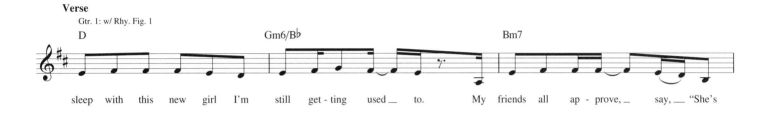

sleep with this new girl I'm still get - ting used __ to. My friends all ap - prove, __ say, __ "She's

gon - na be good for you." They throw me

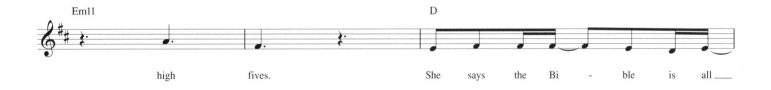

high fives. She says the Bi - ble is all __

__ that she reads __ and pre - fers __ that I __ not use pro - fan - i -

D.S. al Coda

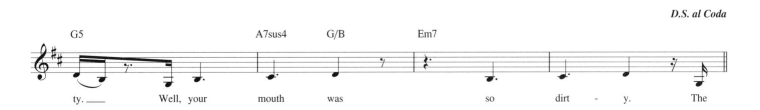

ty. __ Well, your mouth was so dirt - y. The

$\oplus$ Coda

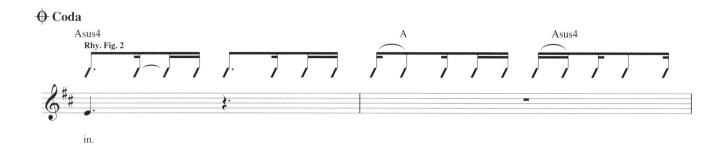

in.

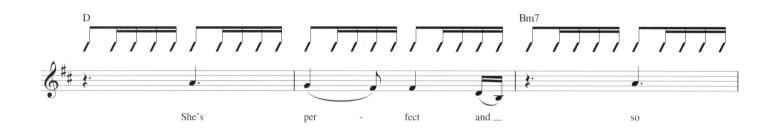

She's   per - fect   and __   so

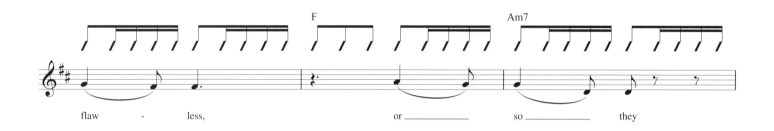

flaw - less,   or _____   so _____   they

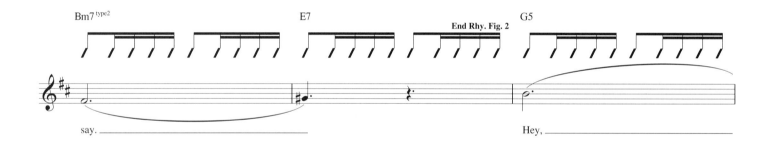

say. _____   Hey, _____

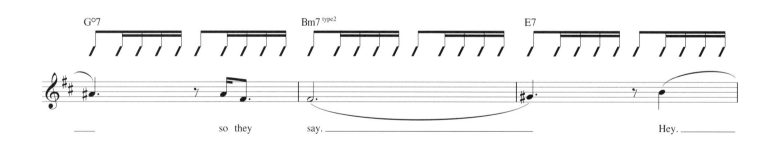

____   so they   say. _____   Hey. _____

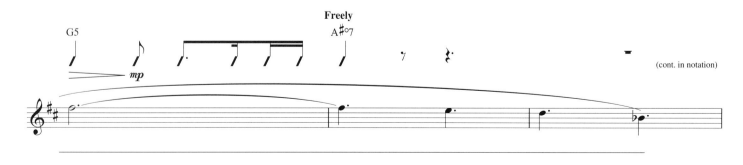

(cont. in notation)

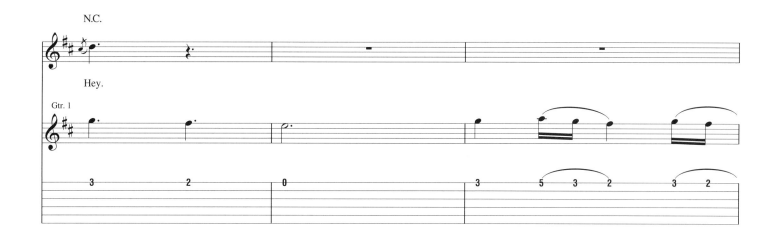

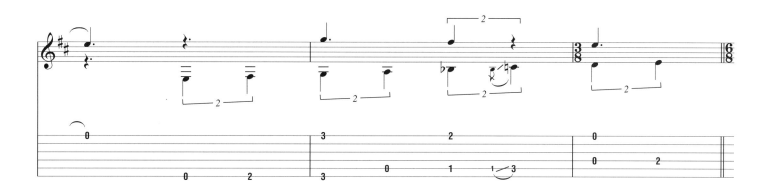

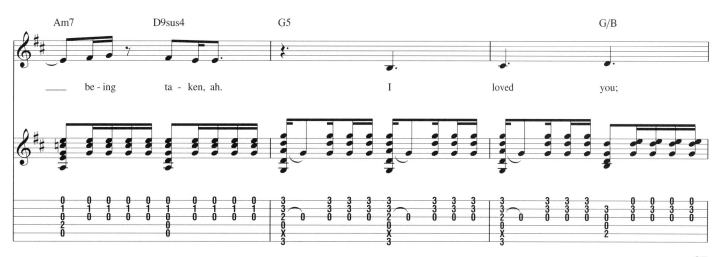

gray   sweat   pants,   no

make - up,   so   per - fect. _____

(cont. in slashes)

Chorus

Gtr. 1

_____ Our   love   was   com - fort -

'ble _____ and   so   bro - ken _____

Gtr. 1: w/ Rhy. Fig. 2

in. _____   She's   per - fect, _____

so   flaw - less, _____   and no, no, _____ I'm

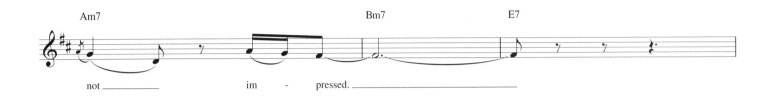

not _____   im - pressed. _____

No, ___   I ___ want you ___ back, ___   back. _____

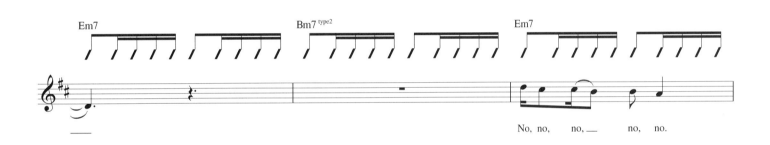

No, no,   no, ___ no, no.

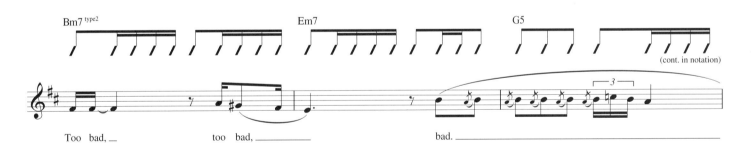

Too bad, ___   too bad, _____   bad. _____

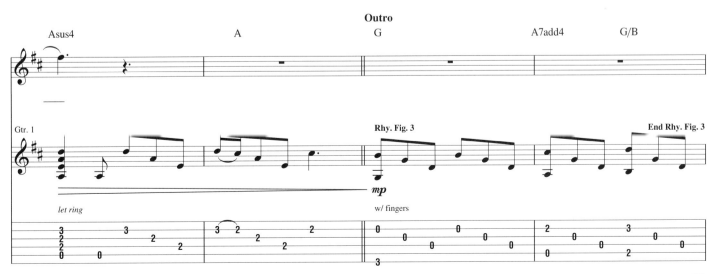

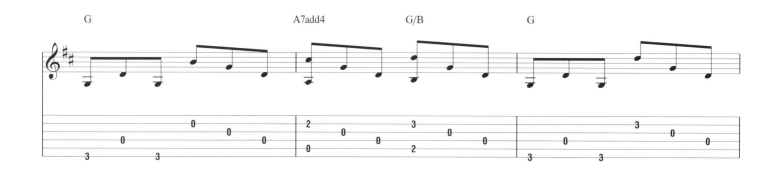

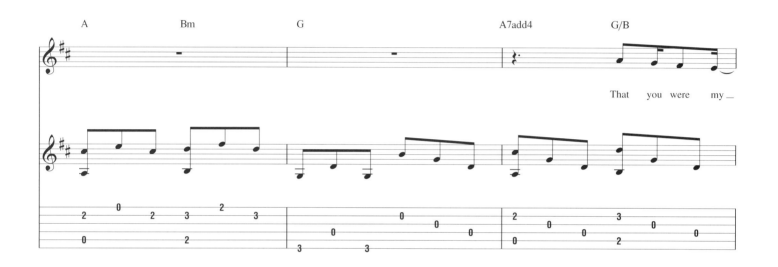

That you were my ___

Gtr. 1: w/ Rhy. Fig. 3 (12 times)

___ first love ___ is just dumb luck,

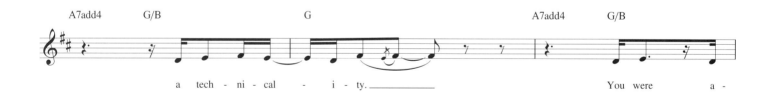

a tech - ni - cal - i - ty. ___ You were a-

head of me. ___ That you were my first love

is just dumb, ___ dumb, ___ stu - pid ___ luck, ___ a tech - ni -

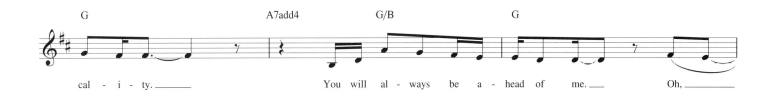

cal - i - ty. _____ You will al - ways be a - head of me. _____ Oh, _____

_____ oh, _____ tell me why I have _____ to

prac - tice on you, why I

have to prac - tice on _____ your heart.

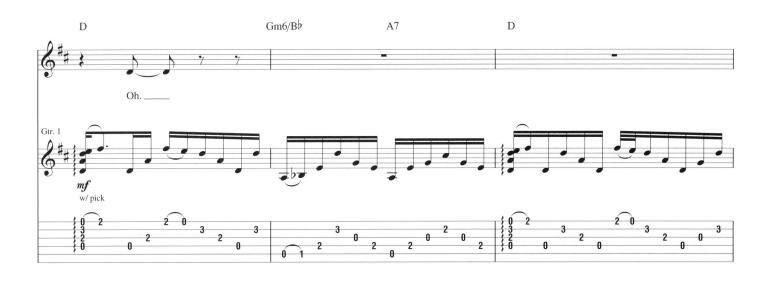

Oh. _____

Gtr. 1

mf
w/ pick

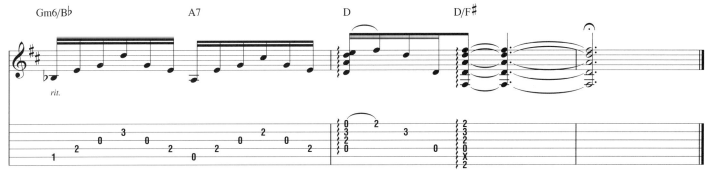

rit.

COVERED IN RAIN

Words and Music by
John Mayer

*T = thumb on 6th string

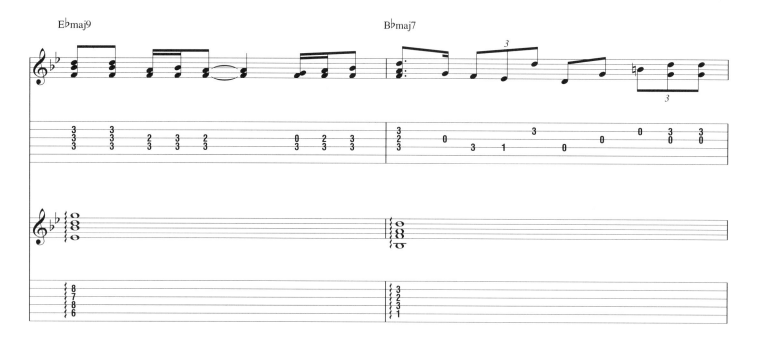

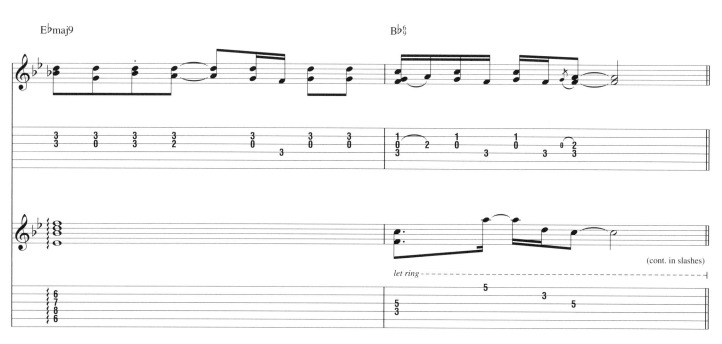

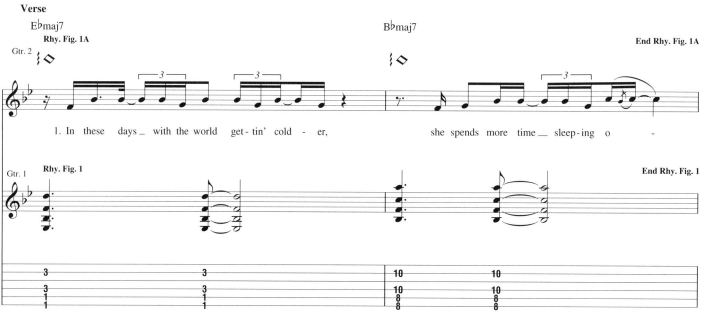

1. In these days ___ with the world get-tin' cold - er, she spends more time ___ sleep-ing o - -

Chorus

rain,   rain, _____   when I'm cov-ered in _____

_____ rain,   rain,   rain,   rain. _____

Interlude

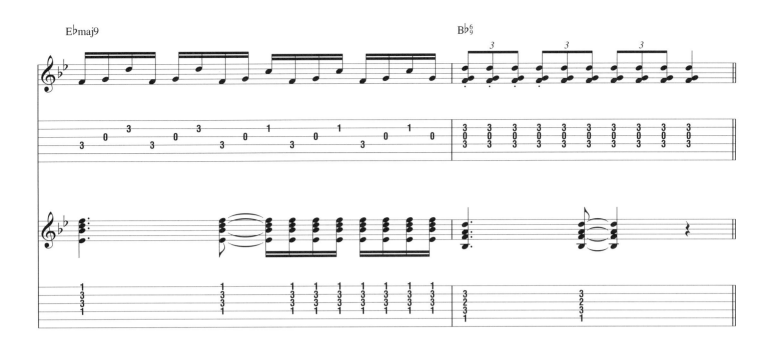

Verse

Gtr. 1: w/ Rhy. Fig. 1 (2 times)
Gtr. 2: w/ Rhy. Fig. 1A

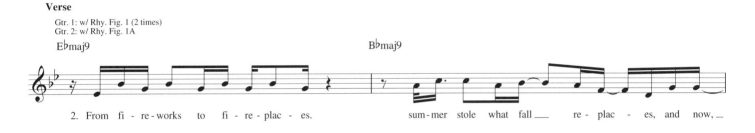

2. From fi-re-works to fi-re-plac-es. sum-mer stole what fall ___ re-plac-es, and now, ___

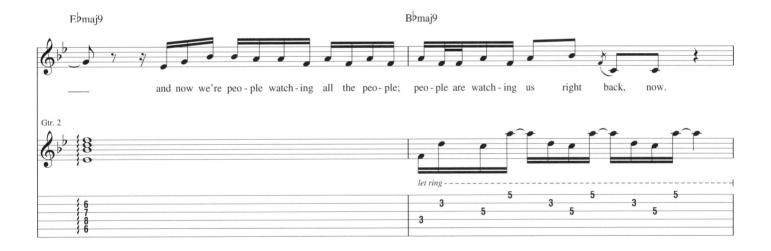

___ and now we're peo-ple watch-ing all the peo-ple; peo-ple are watch-ing us right back, now.

Gtr. 2: w/ Rhy. Fig. 1A

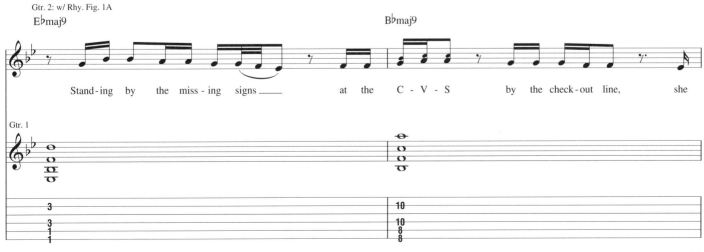

Stand-ing by the miss-ing signs ___ at the C - V - S by the check-out line, she

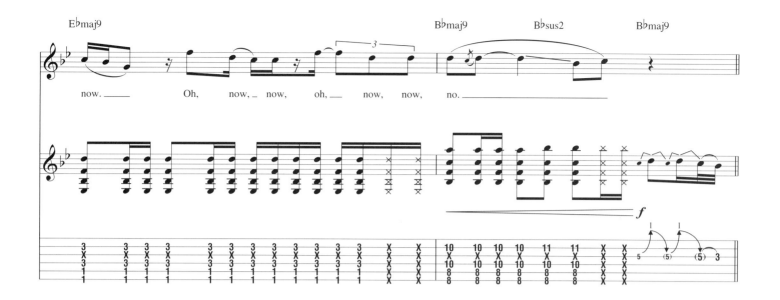

Guitar Solo

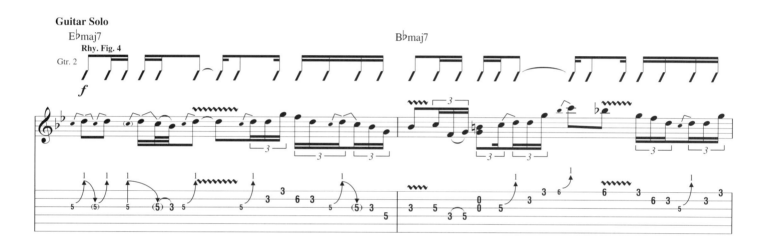

Gtr. 2: w/ Rhy. Fig. 4

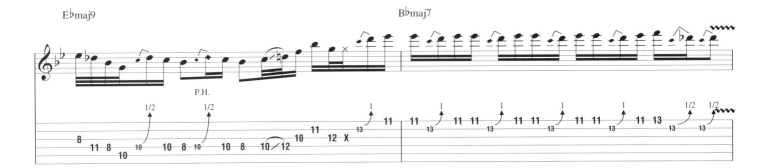

Gtr. 2: w/ Rhy. Fig. 3 (6 times)

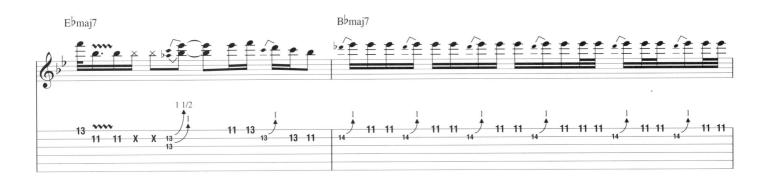

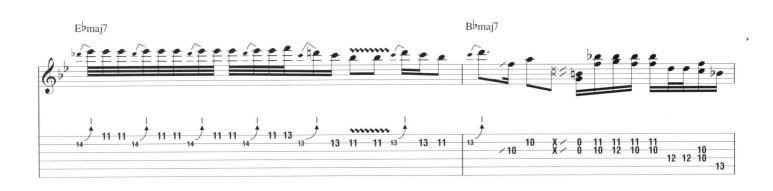

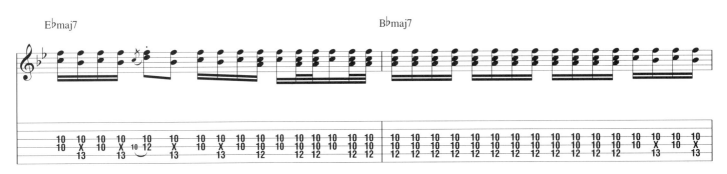

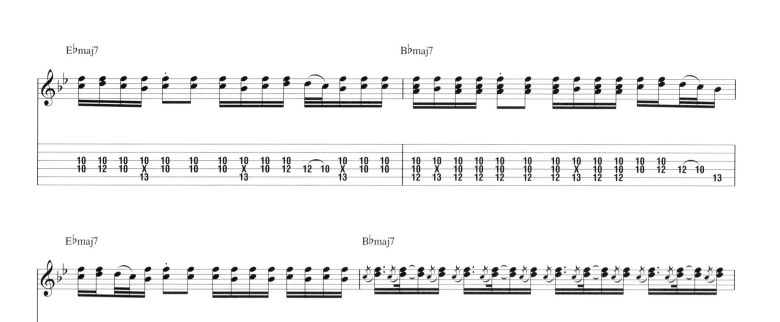

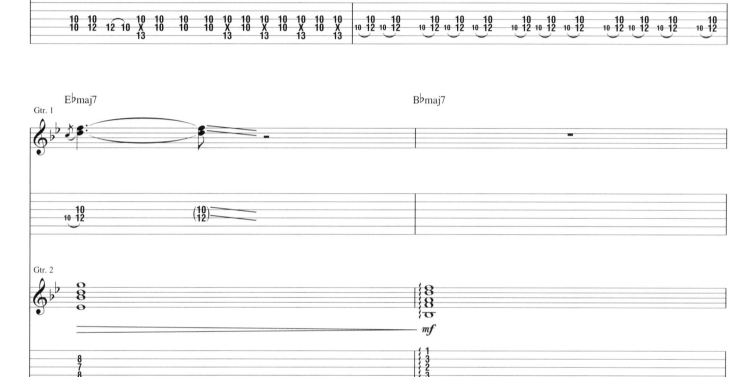

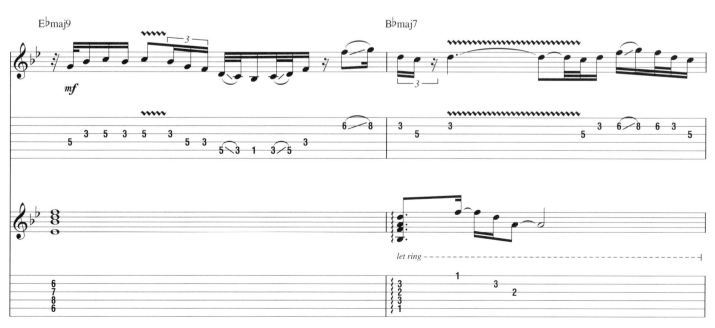

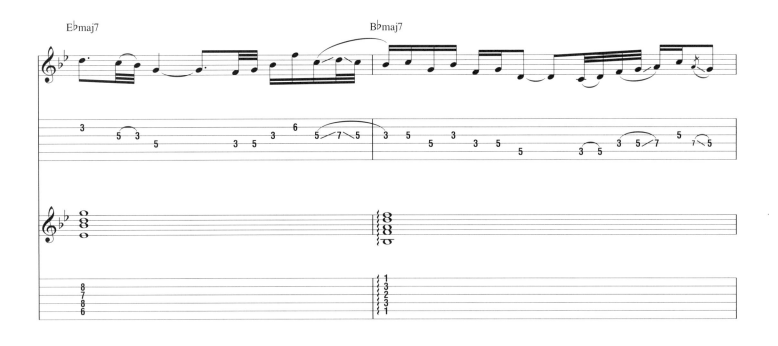

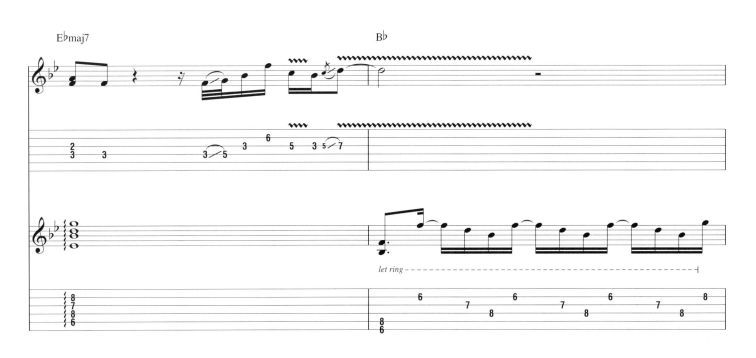

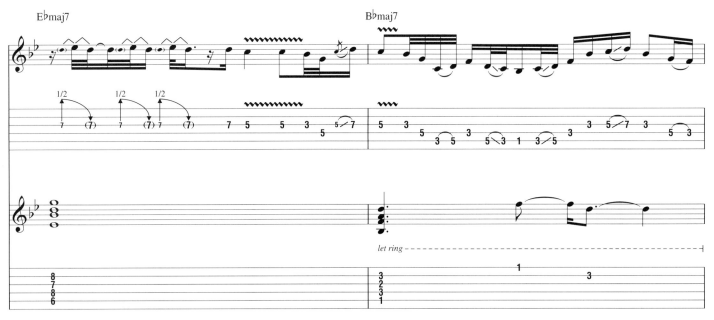

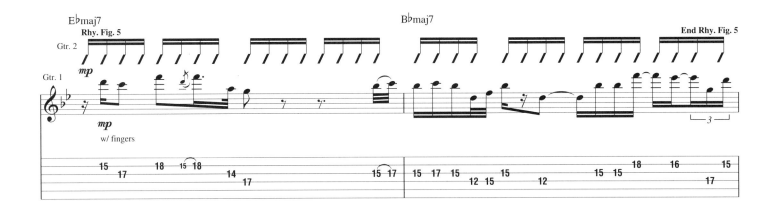

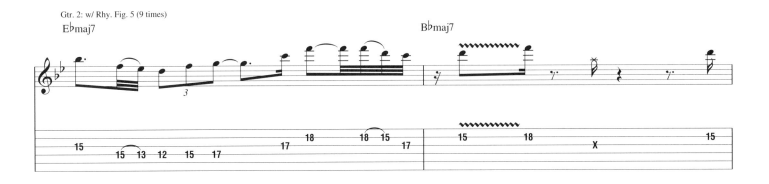

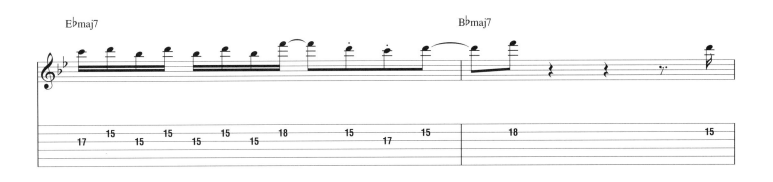

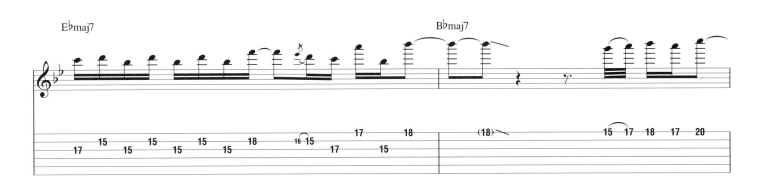

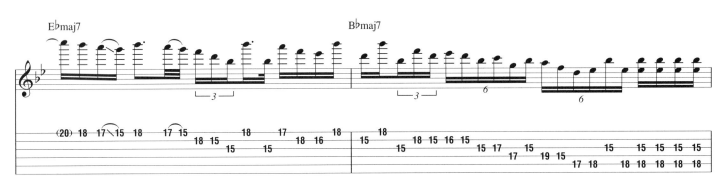

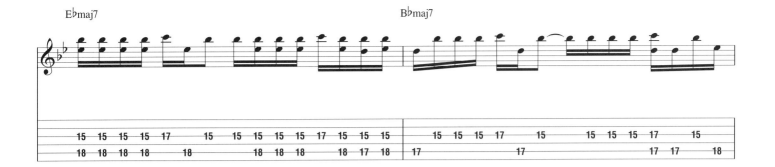

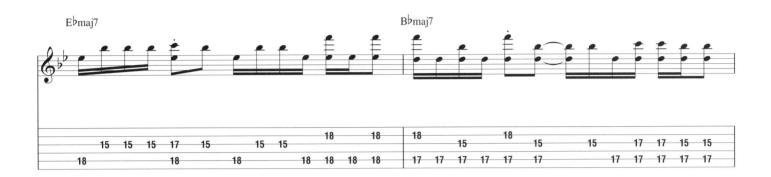

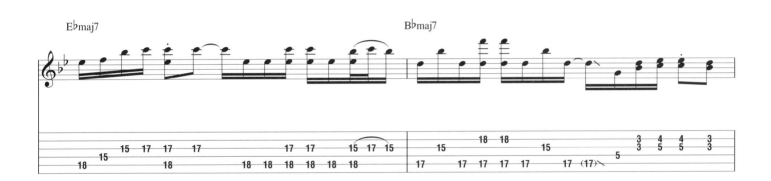

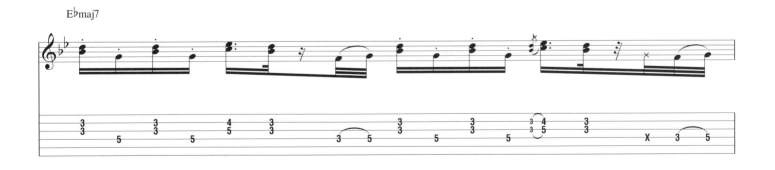

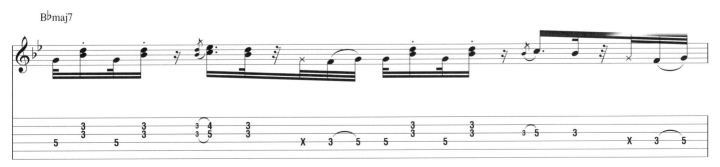

Ebmaj7

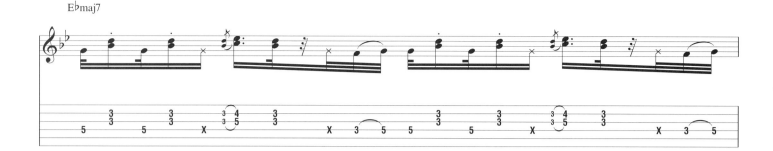

Bbmaj7

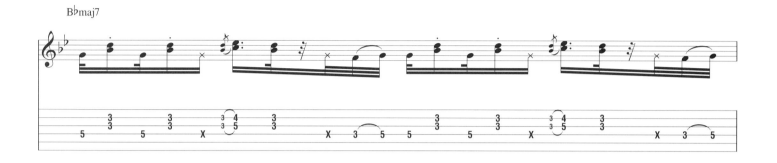

Ebmaj7

Gtr. 2

grad. cresc.

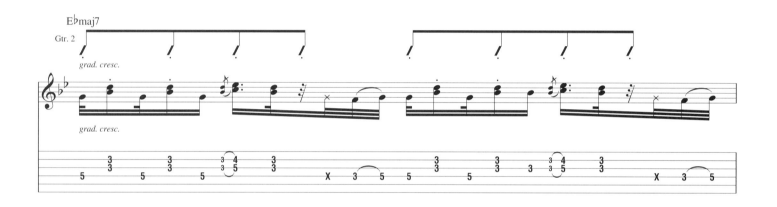

grad. cresc.

Bbmaj7

Ebmaj9

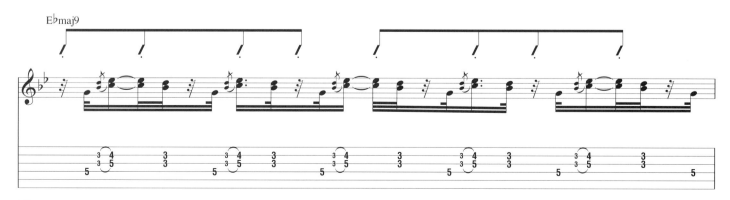

Gtr. 2: w/ Rhy. Fig. 6

E♭maj7

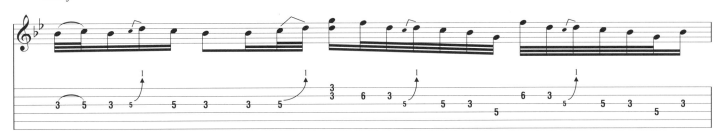

B♭maj7

E♭maj7

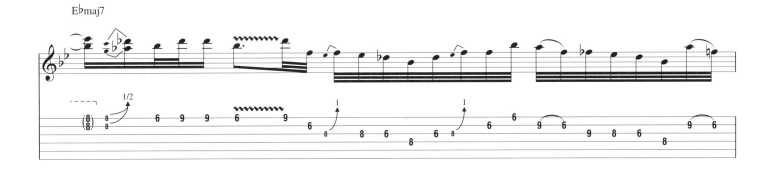

B♭maj9

Gtr. 2

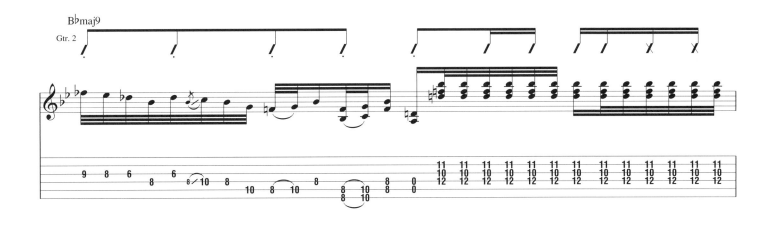

E♭maj7

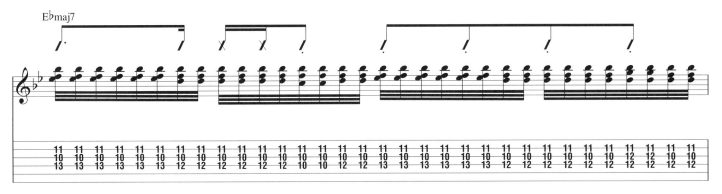

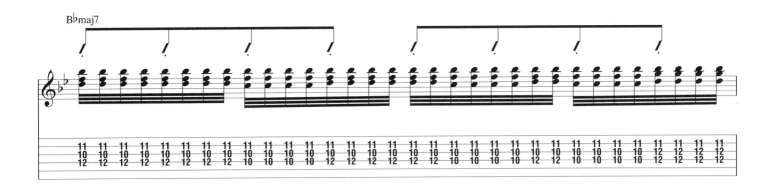

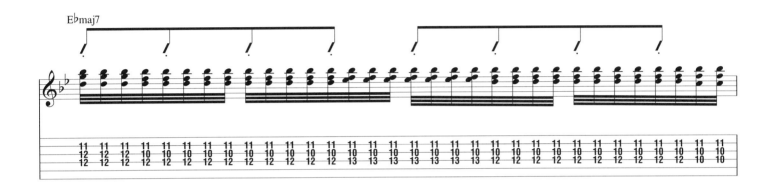

End double-time feel

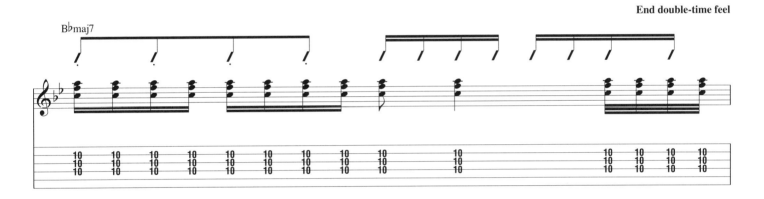

Gtr. 2: w/ Rhy. Fig. 3 (3 times)

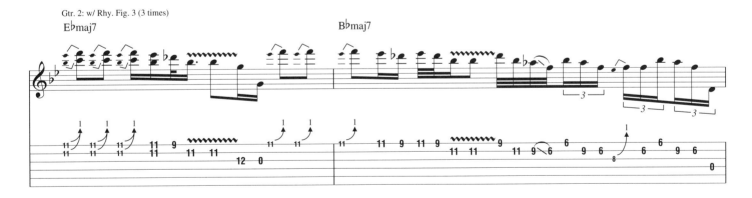

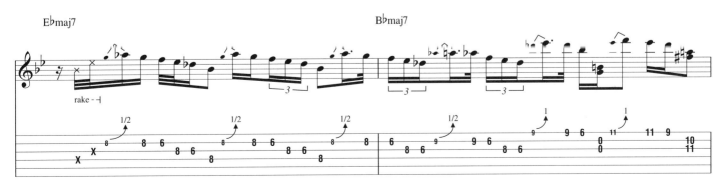

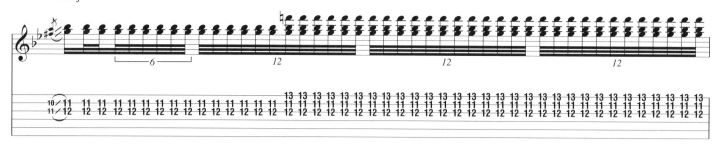

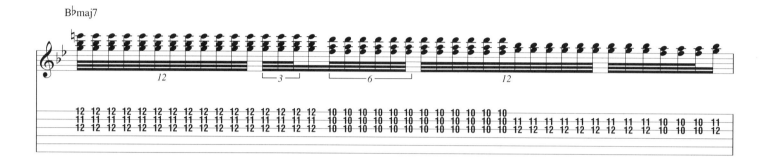

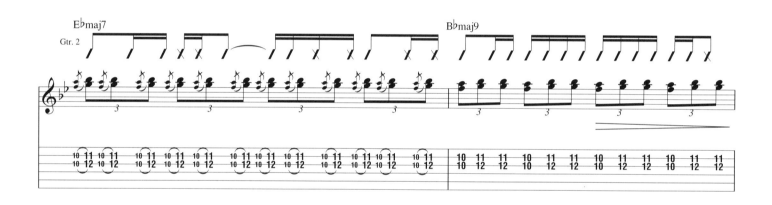

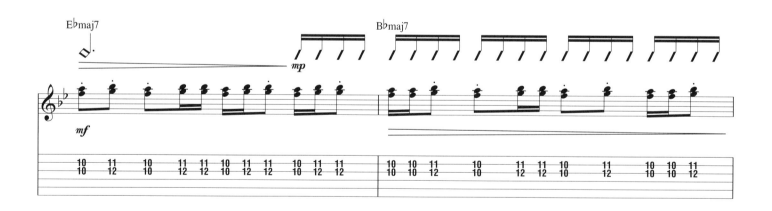

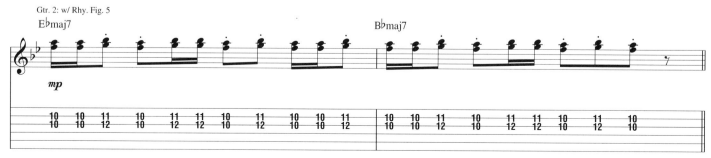

Verse

Gtr. 1 tacet
Gtr. 2: w/ Rhy. Fig. 5 (3 times)

3. And come De - cem - ber, Lyd - i - a left. She men - tioned some - thing 'bout it be - ing for _____ the best, _____

and I can't say I dis - a - gree, and it's kill - ing me.

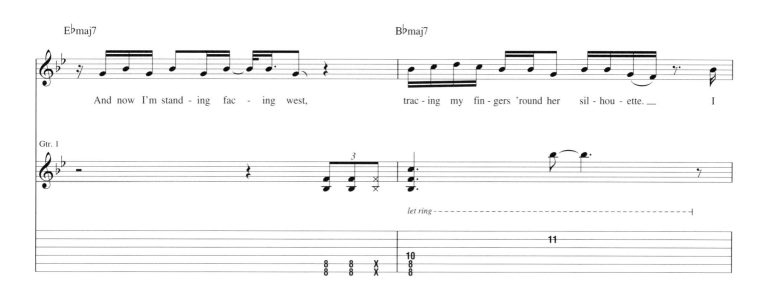

And now I'm stand - ing fac - i - ng west, trac - ing my fin - gers 'round her sil - hou - ette. _____ I

have - n't got - ten used _____ to you, but it's the best thing I got when I'm cov - ered _____ in

Chorus

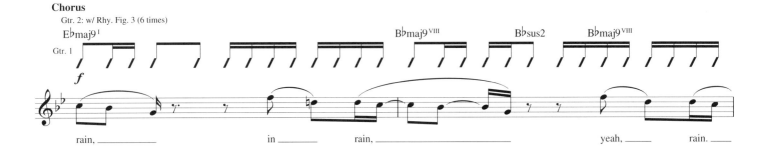

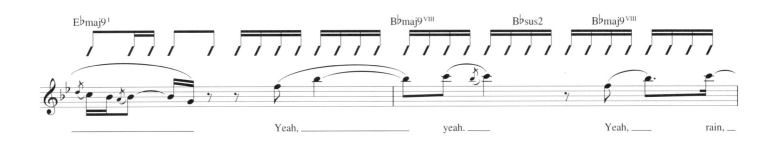

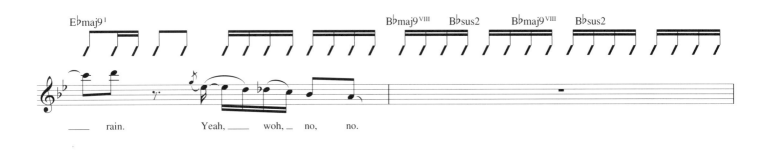

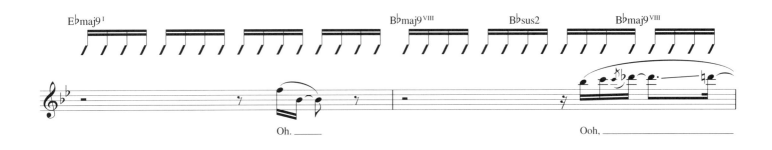

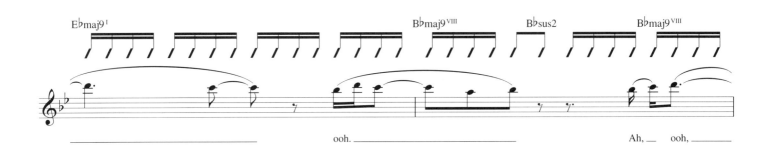

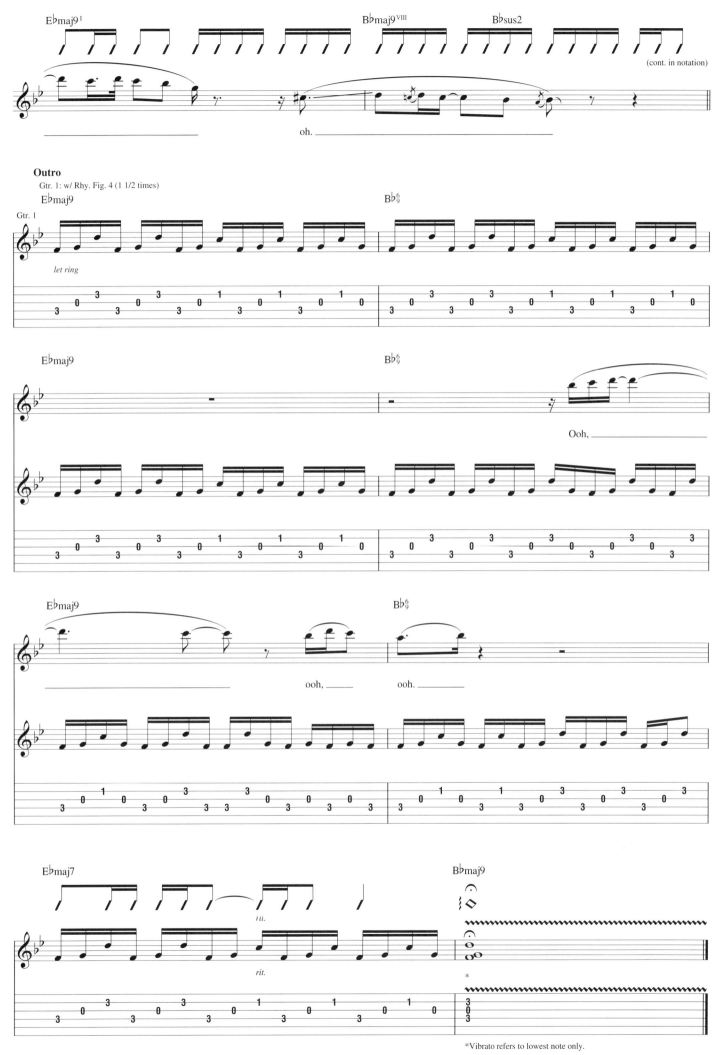

*Vibrato refers to lowest note only.

EVERY DAY I HAVE THE BLUES

Words and Music by
Peter Chatman

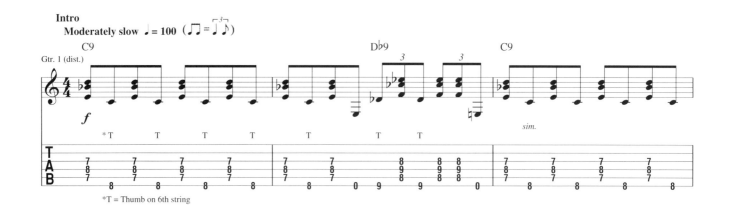

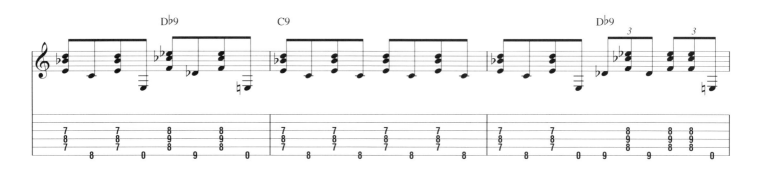

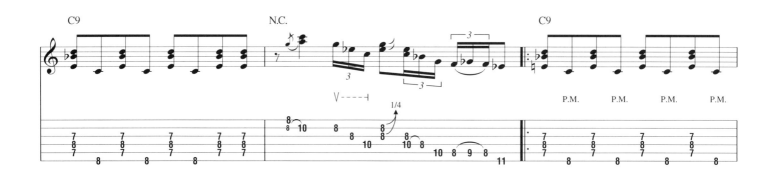

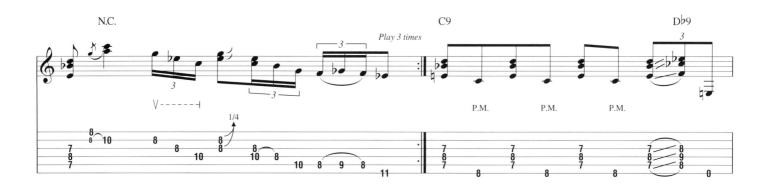

Guitar Solo

*Chord symbols reflect implied harmony (till 3rd verse).

w/ wah-wah as filter

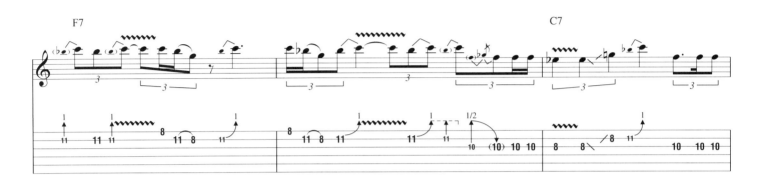

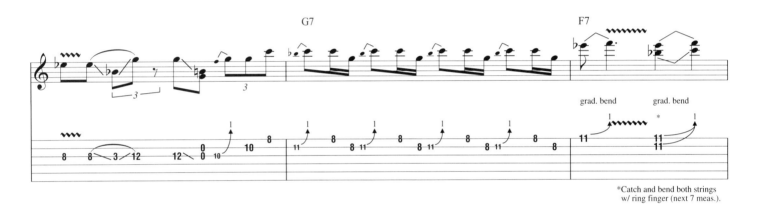

*Catch and bend both strings
w/ ring finger (next 7 meas.).

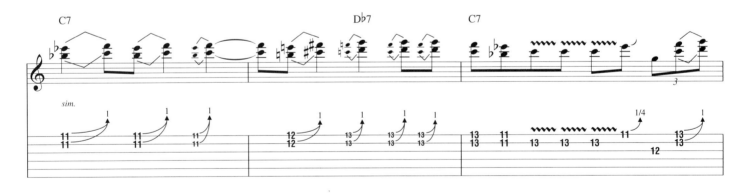

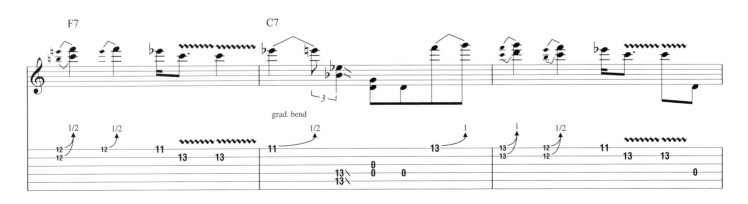

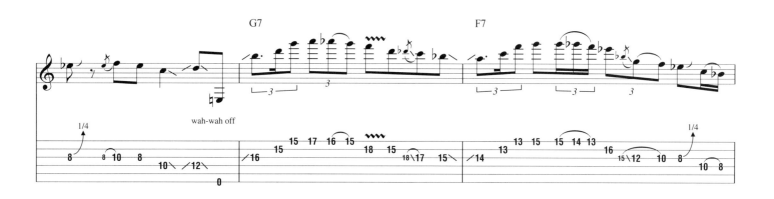

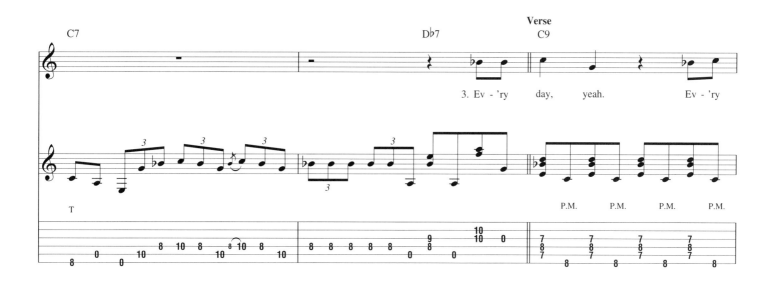

3. Ev - 'ry   day,   yeah.   Ev - 'ry

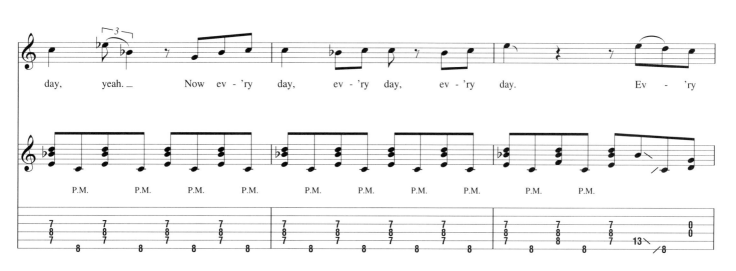

day,   yeah. __   Now ev - 'ry   day,   ev - 'ry   day,   ev - 'ry   day.   Ev - 'ry

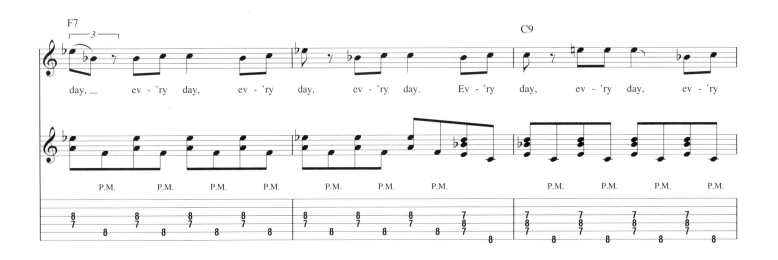

day, — ev-'ry day, ev-'ry day, ev-'ry day. Ev-'ry day, ev-'ry day, ev-'ry

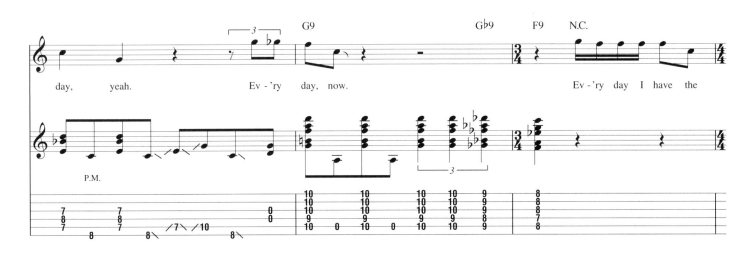

day, yeah. Ev-'ry day, now. Ev-'ry day I have the

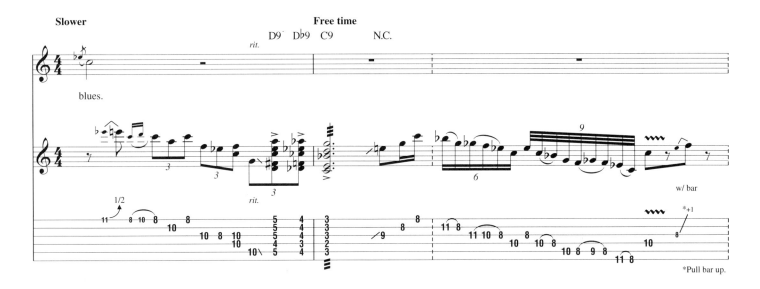

blues.

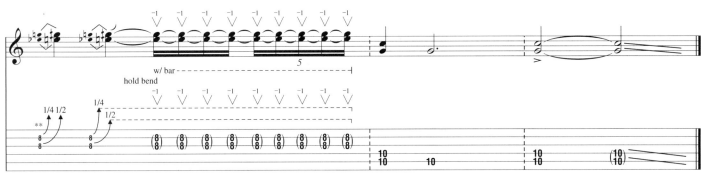

**Bend both strings toward floor w/ index finger.

GOOD LOVE IS ON THE WAY

Words and Music by
John Mayer, Pino Paladino
and Steven Jordan

*T = Thumb on 6th string

Moderately slow ♩ = 100

Play 6 times

Verse

1. I'm a la - zy lov - er, un - der - cov -

**Chord symbols reflect basic harmony.

- er, wast - ing time.

Then one day _____ this sum - mer, I changed my num -

- ber _____ to cut my _____ line. _____

Chorus

Good love is on _____ the way.

I've been

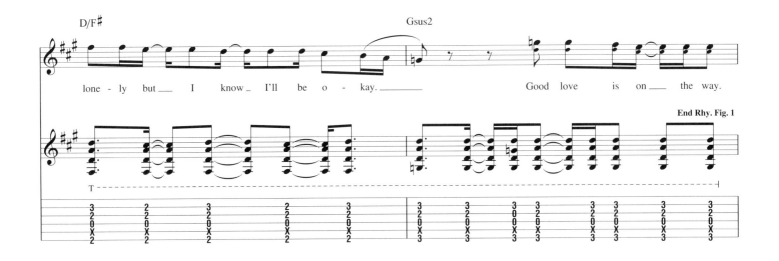

lone - ly but __ I know __ I'll be o - kay. _____   Good love is on __ the way.

End Rhy. Fig. 1

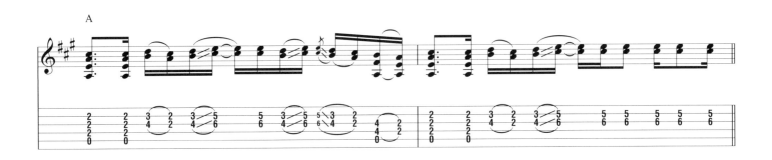

Verse

2. Three years   I've __ been bro - ken - heart - ed. _____   Now   I know __ her ghost __

slight P.M. - - - - - - - - - - - - - - - - -

__ is   fi - n'lly gone. __

slight P.M. - - - - - - - - - - - - - - - - -   let ring -

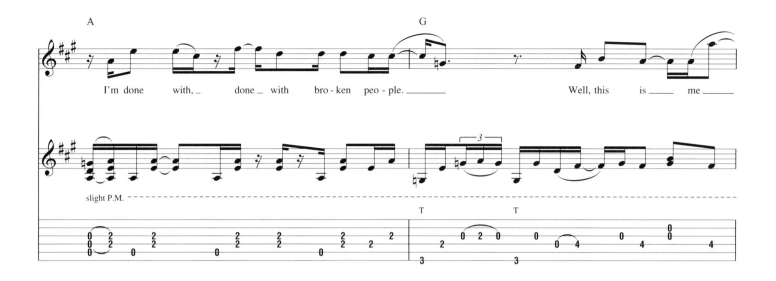

A   G

I'm done with, _ done _ with bro - ken peo - ple. _____   Well, this is _____ me _____

slight P.M.

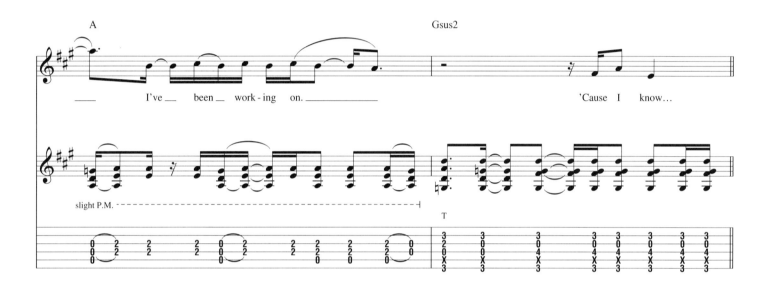

A   Gsus2

_____ I've _ been _ work - ing on. _____   'Cause I know...

slight P.M.

Chorus
Gtr. 1: w/ Rhy. Fig. 1

D/F#   Gsus2

Good love in on _____ the way.

A

Oh, I've been lone -

D/F#   Gsus2

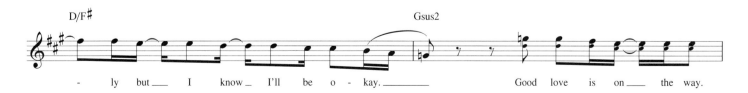

- ly but ___ I know ___ I'll be o - kay. _____ Good love is on ___ the way.

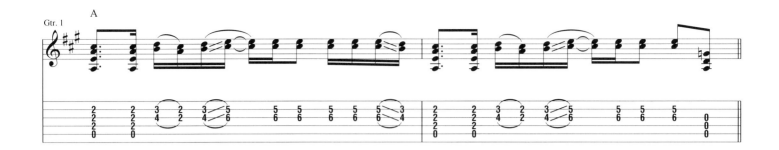

Bridge

Good to go for wher-ev-er I'm need-ed.

let ring

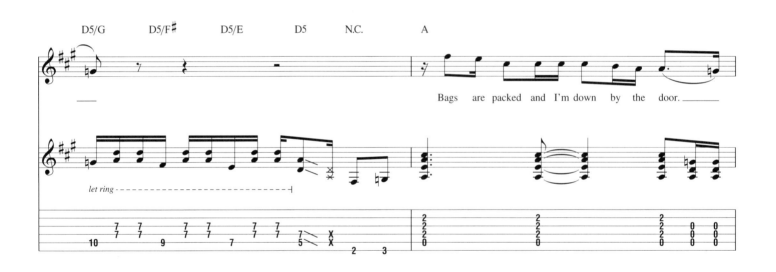

Bags are packed and I'm down by the door.

let ring

You can take all the tricks up my sleeve; I don't

let ring

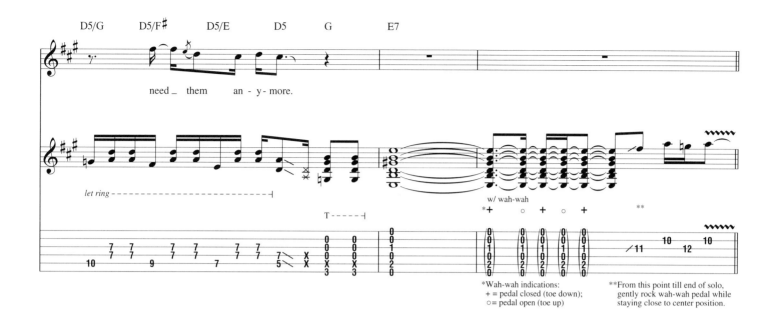

*Wah-wah indications:
+ = pedal closed (toe down);
○ = pedal open (toe up)

**From this point till end of solo,
gently rock wah-wah pedal while
staying close to center position.

Guitar Solo

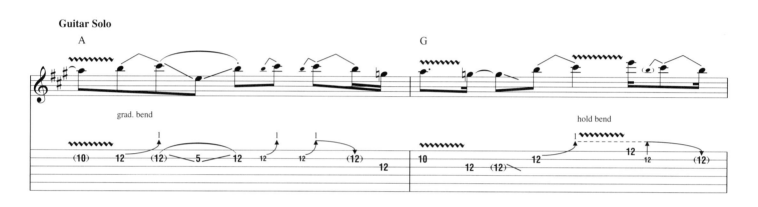

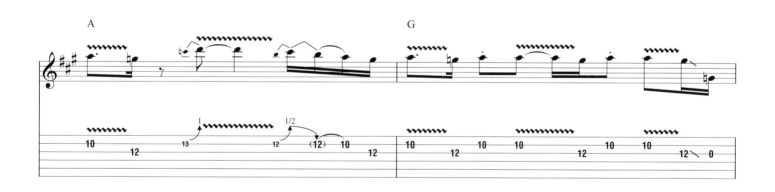

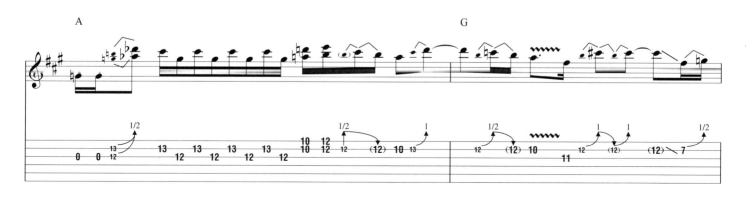

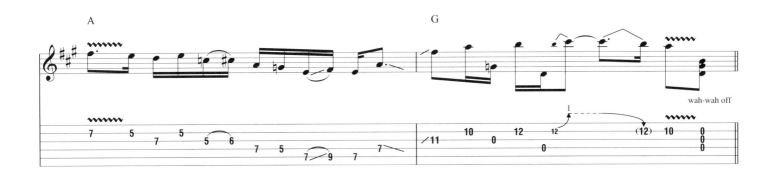

Chorus

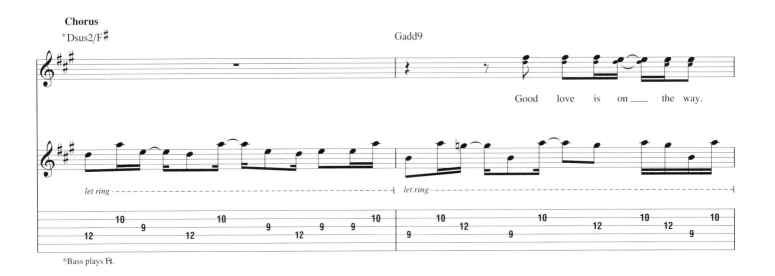

Good love is on ___ the way.

*Bass plays F♯.

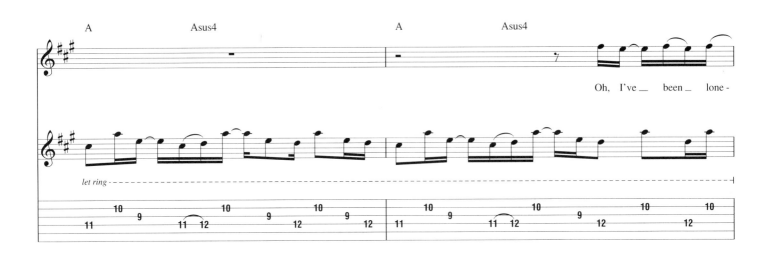

Oh, I've ___ been ___ lone -

- ly but I know ___ I'll be o - kay. ___ Good love is on ___ the way.

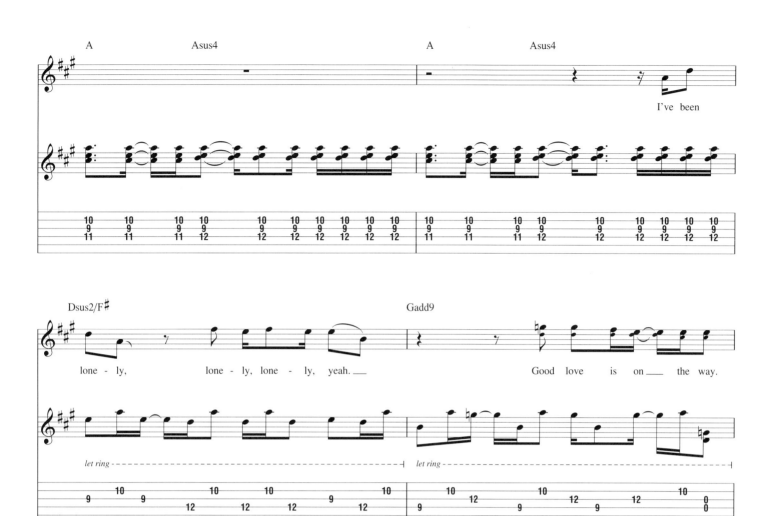

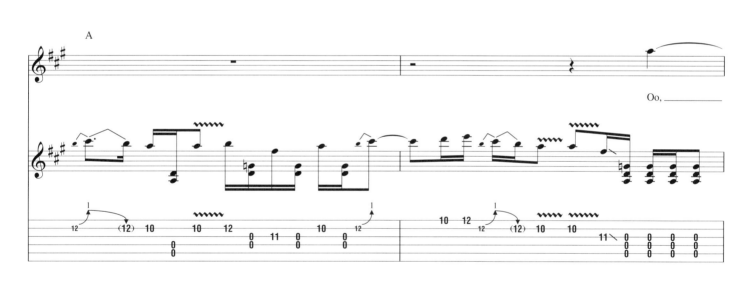

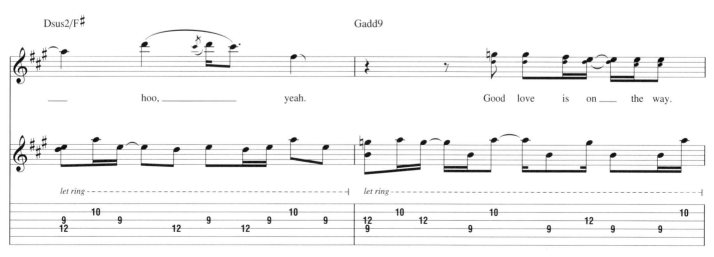

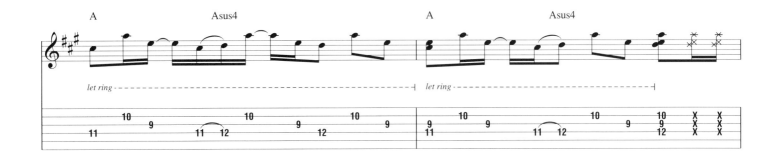

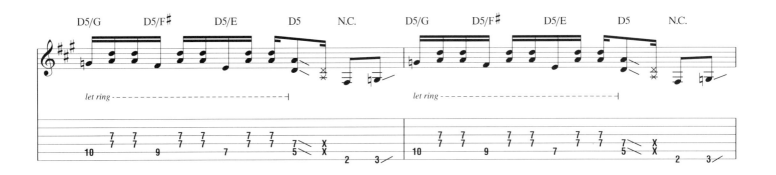

*Using a gtr. w/ Stratocaster-style electronics, quickly move pickup selector back and forth between neck and bridge positions.

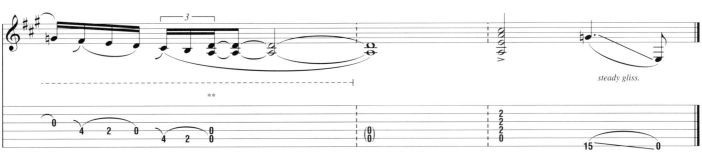

**Open 4th string sounded by index finger during pull-off; don't pick.

GRAVITY

Words and Music by
John Mayer

Intro
Free time

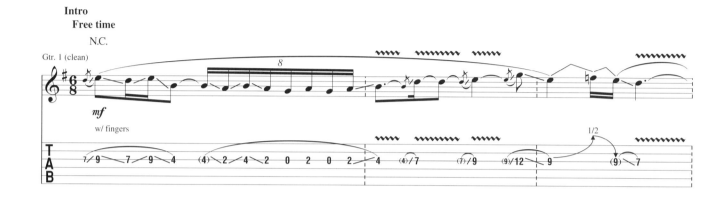

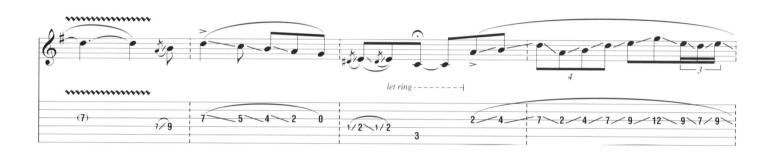

*T = Thumb on
6th string

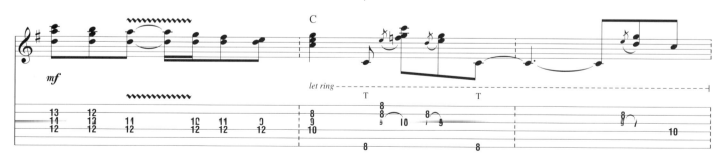

I got d - reams

to re - mem , to re - mem - ber. Oh, grav - i - ty. Oh,

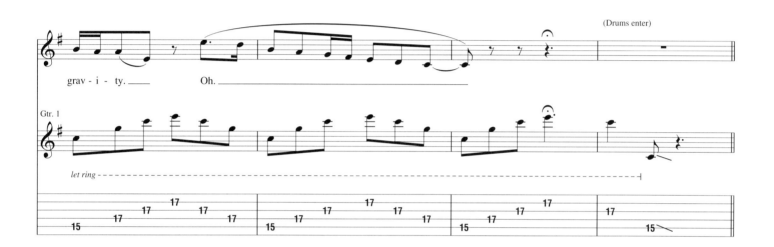

grav - i - ty. _____ Oh.

(Drums enter)

Gtr. 1

let ring -

*Chord symbols reflect overall harmony.

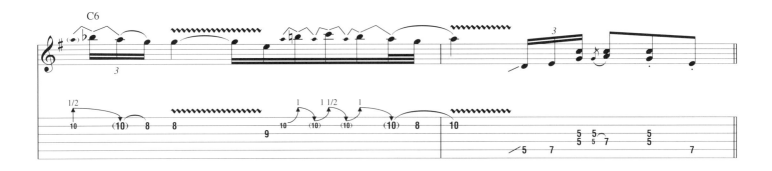

Verse

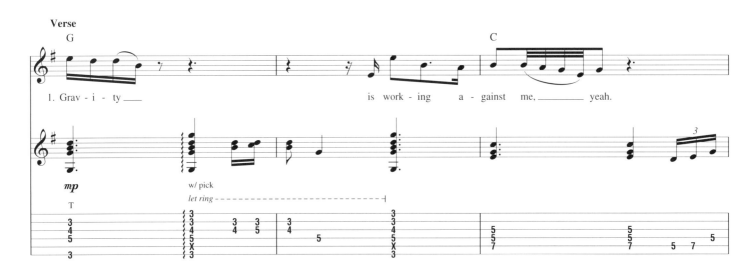

1. Grav - i - ty _____ is work - ing a - gainst me, _____ yeah.

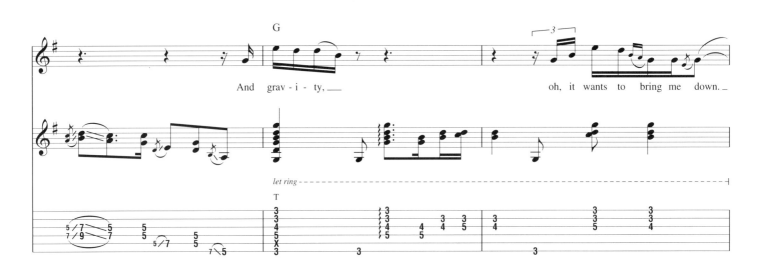

And grav - i - ty, ___ oh, it wants to bring me down. _

𝄋 **Chorus**

Oh, I'll nev - er know what
twice as much ain't

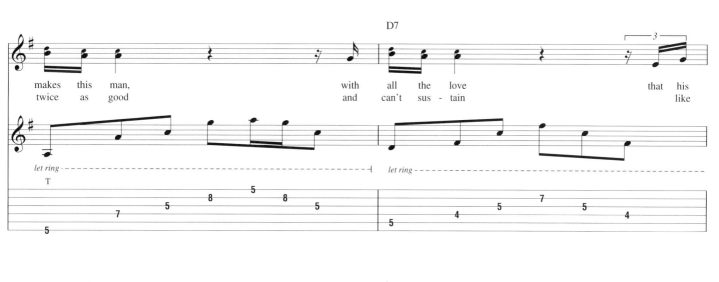

makes this man,   with all the love   that his
twice as good   and can't sus - tain   like

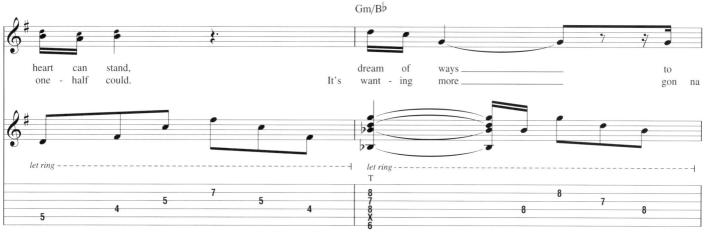

heart can stand,   dream of ways _____   to
one - half could.   It's want - ing more _____   gon na

To Coda 1 ⊕
To Coda 2 ⊕

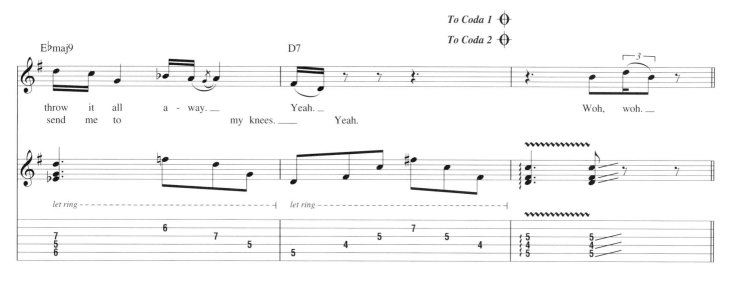

throw it all a - way. ___ Yeah.   Woh, woh. ___
send me to   my knees. ___ Yeah.

Verse

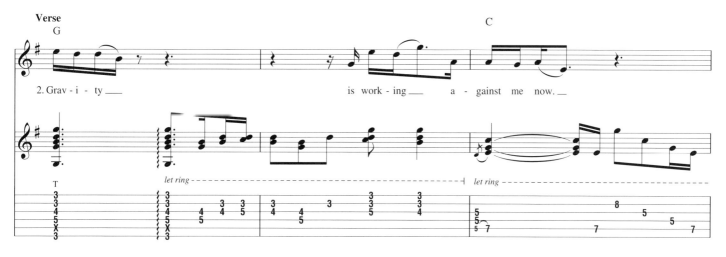

2. Grav - i - ty ___   is work - ing ___ a - gainst me now. ___

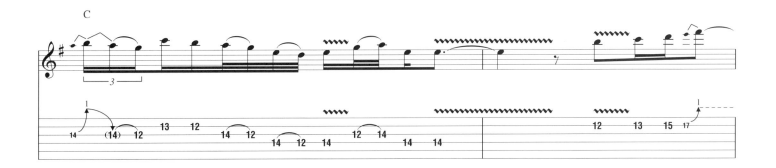

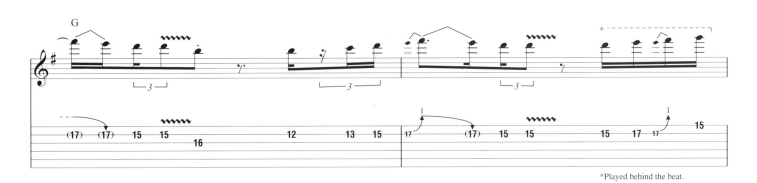

*Played behind the beat.

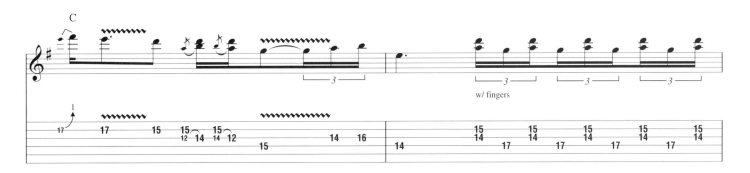

w/ fingers

D.S. al Coda 2
(take 2nd lyrics)

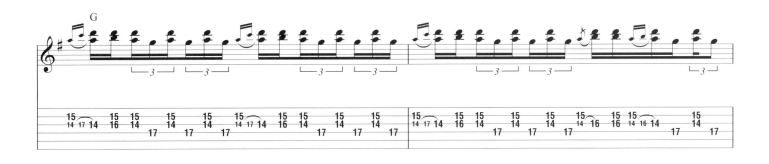

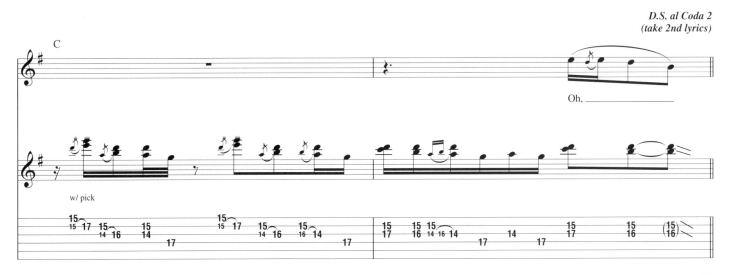

Oh, _____

w/ pick

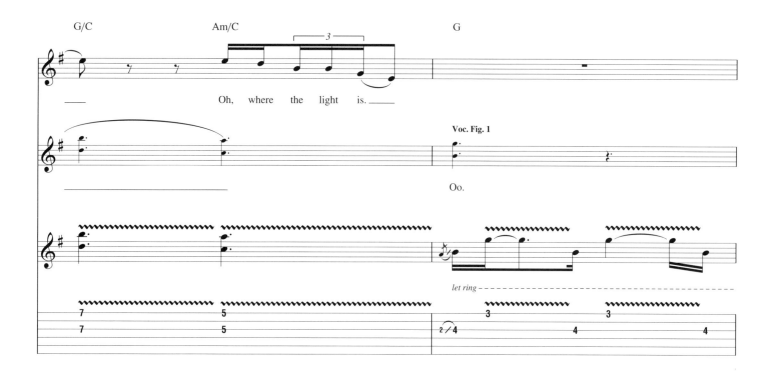

Oh, where the light is.

Voc. Fig. 1

Oo.

let ring ----

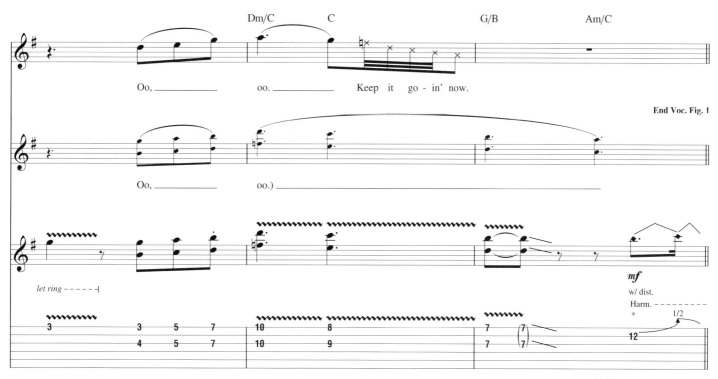

Oo, _____ oo. Keep it go - in' now.

End Voc. Fig. 1

Oo, _____ oo.) _____

let ring -----

mf
w/ dist.
Harm. -------
*

*All bends involving harmonics
are executed by pushing down
on string behind nut.

Outro-Guitar Solo

Bkgd. Voc.: w/ Voc. Fig. 1 (11 times)
Gtr. 2: w/ Riff A (10 times)

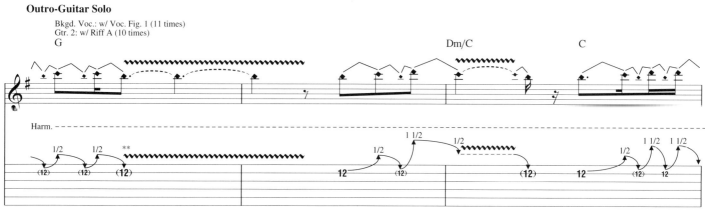

Harm. --------

**All vibrato on harmonics achieved by repeatedly pushing down on string behind nut and releasing.

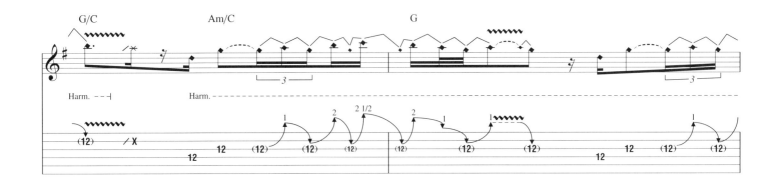

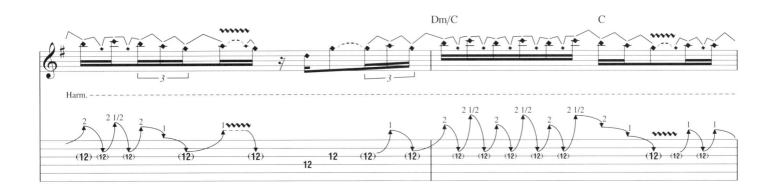

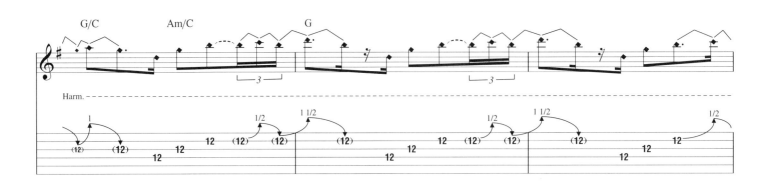

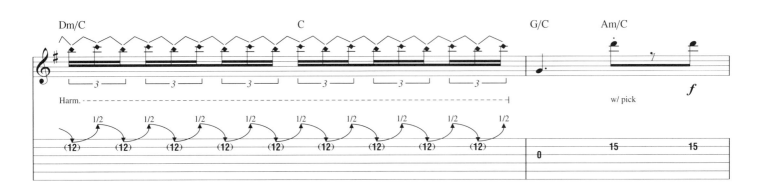

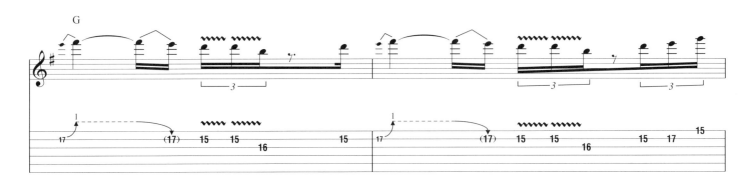

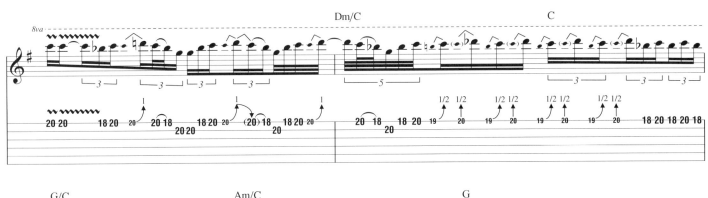

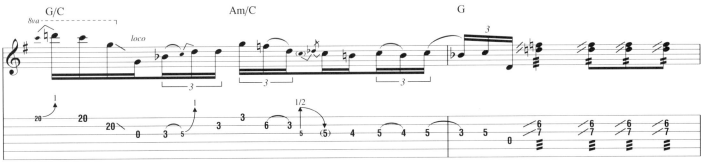

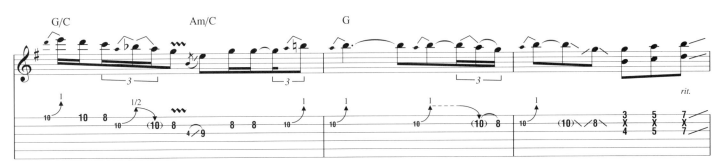

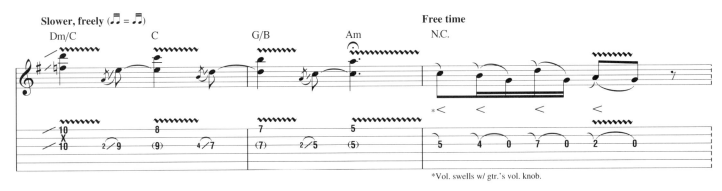

*Vol. swells w/ gtr.'s vol. knob.

Oh,   where   the   light   is. _____

I'M GONNA FIND ANOTHER YOU

Words and Music by
John Mayer

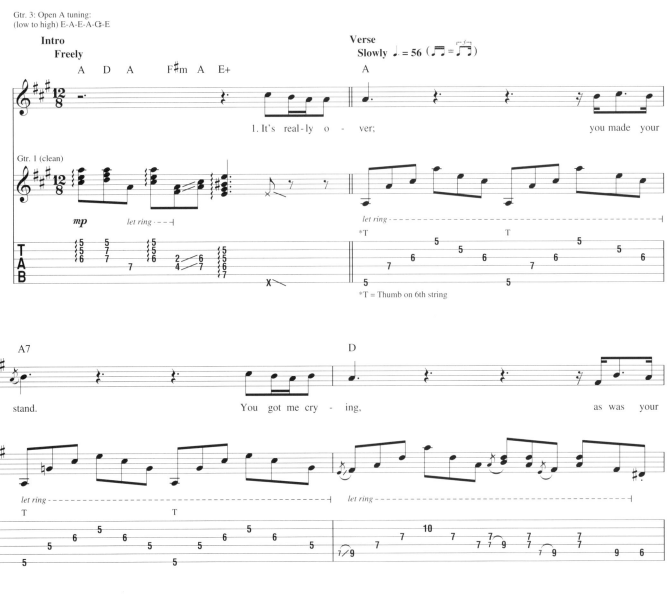

Guitar Solo

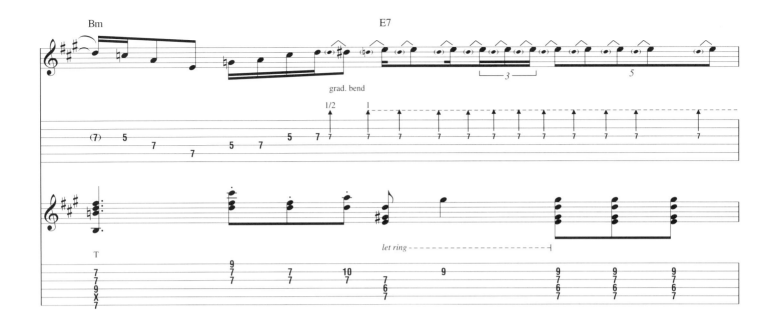

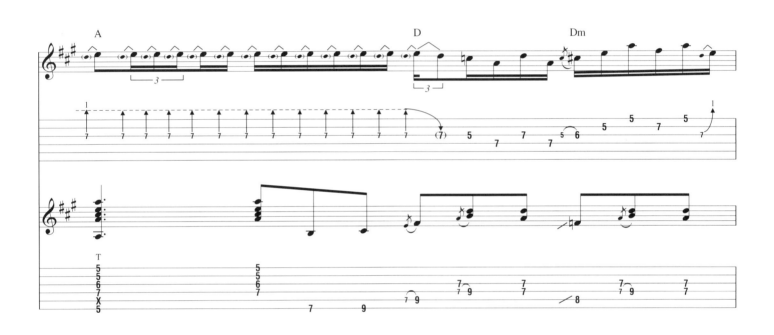

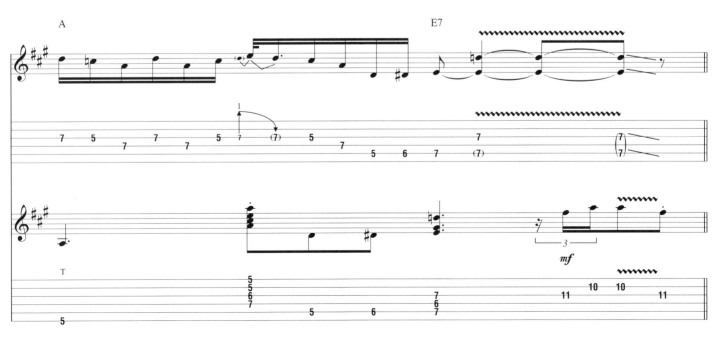

Guitar Solo

Gtr. 2: w/ Rhy. Fig. 1

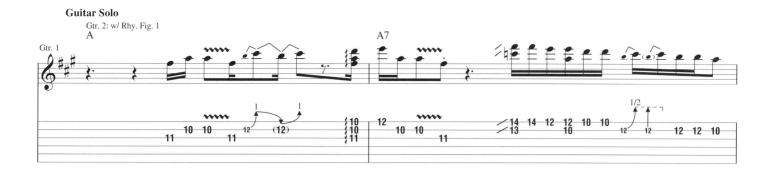

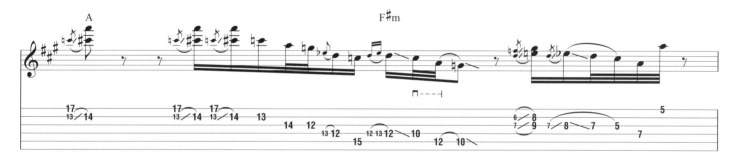

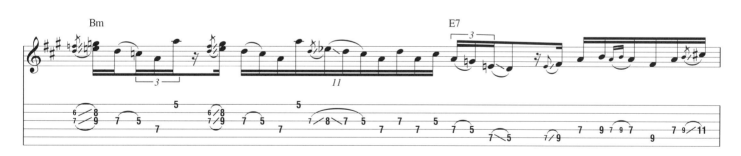

Gtr. 2: w/ Rhy. Fill 1

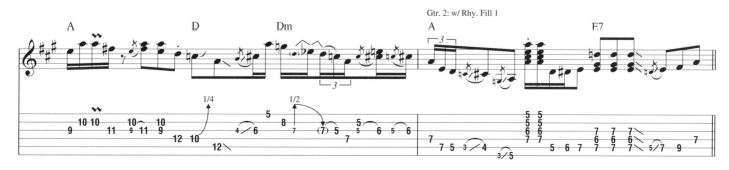

Guitar Solo

Gtr. 1: w/ Rhy. Fig. 1

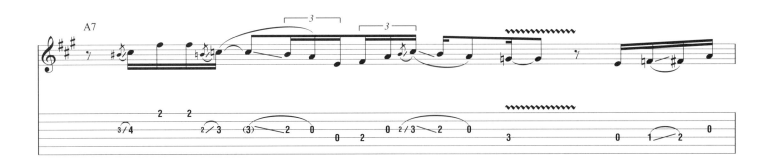

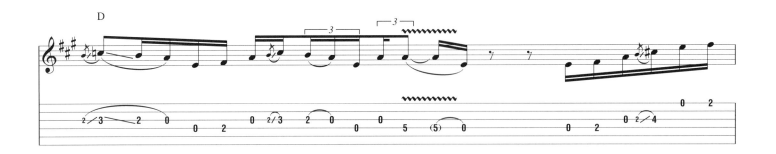

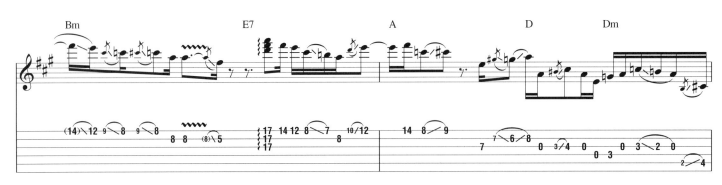

do some things, ___ do some things you would-n't let me do. Oh, ___

oh, ___ al - right, ___ yeah. I'm gon-na find ___ an-oth-er you.

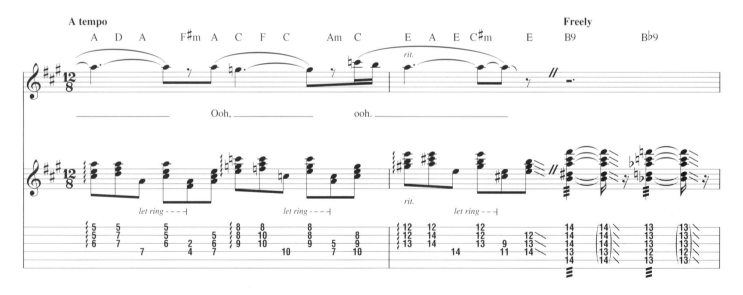

Ooh, ___ ooh.

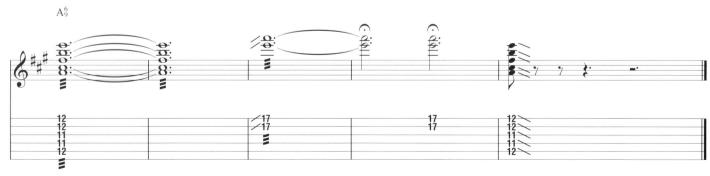

NEON

Words and Music by
John Mayer and Clay Cook

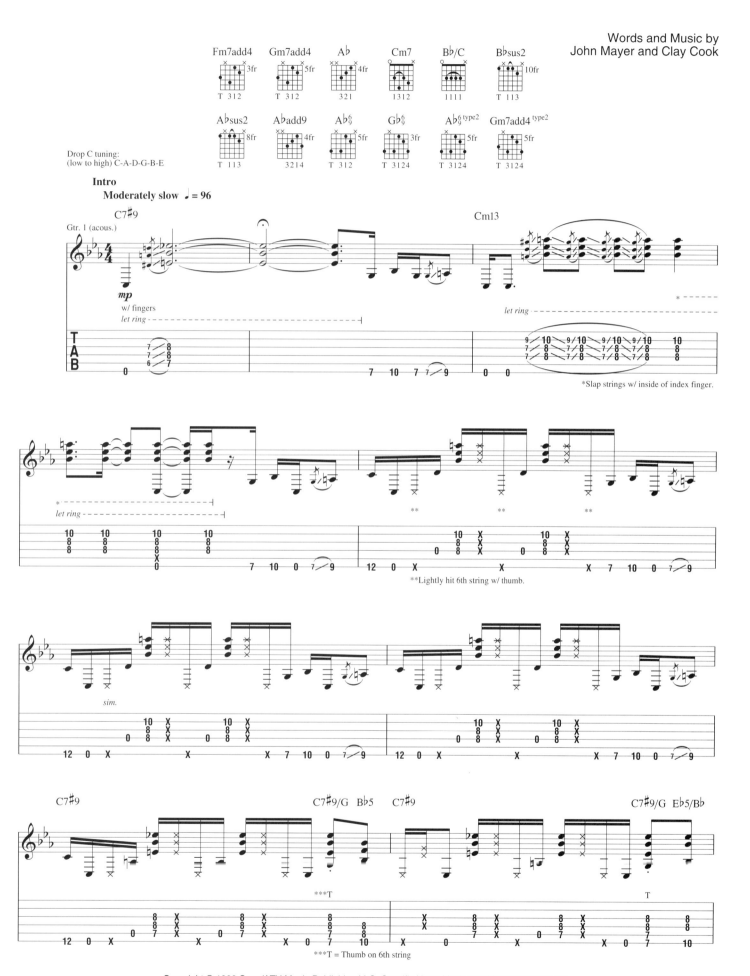

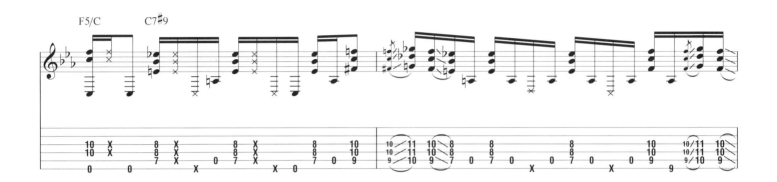

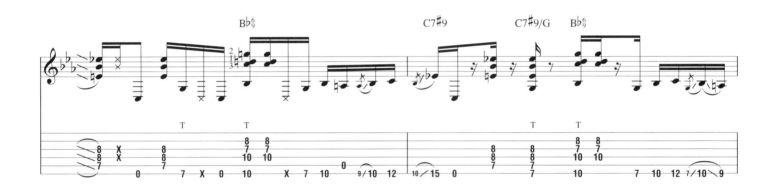

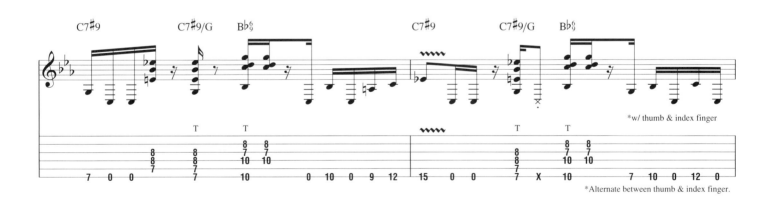

*w/ thumb & index finger

*Alternate between thumb & index finger.

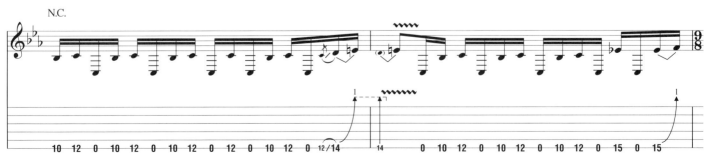

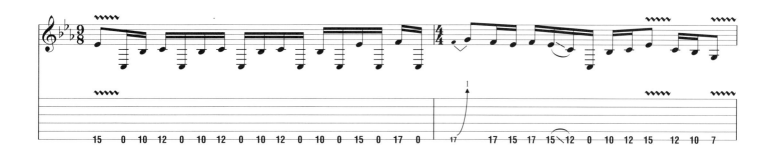

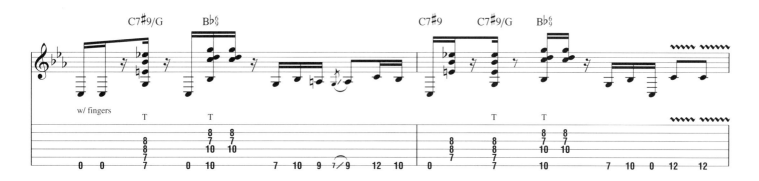

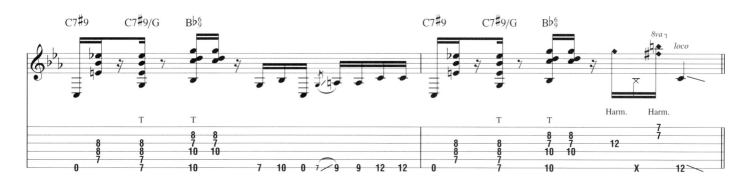

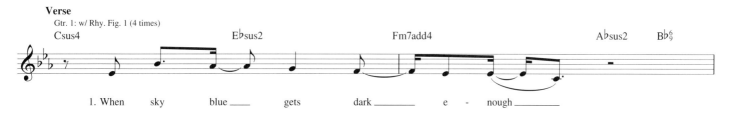

1. When sky blue ___ gets dark ___ e - nough ___

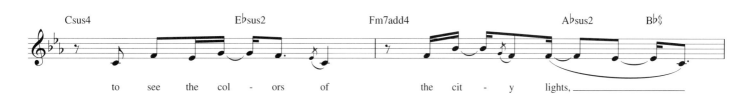

to see the col - ors of the cit - y lights, ___

a trail of ru - by red and dia - mond white _____

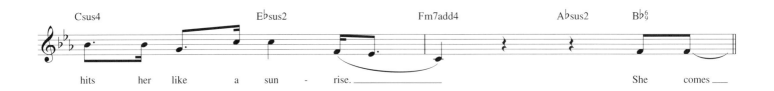

hits her like a sun - rise. _____ She comes _____

Pre-Chorus

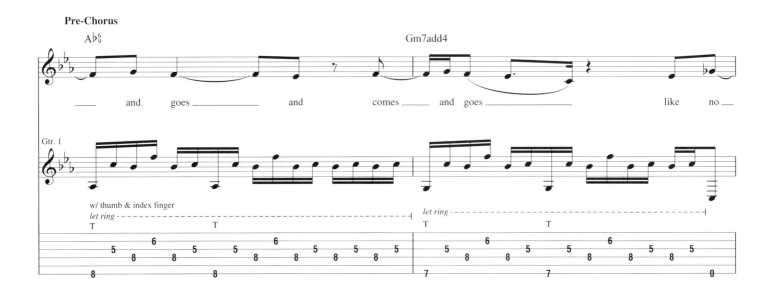

_____ and goes _____ and comes _____ and goes _____ like no

w/ thumb & index finger

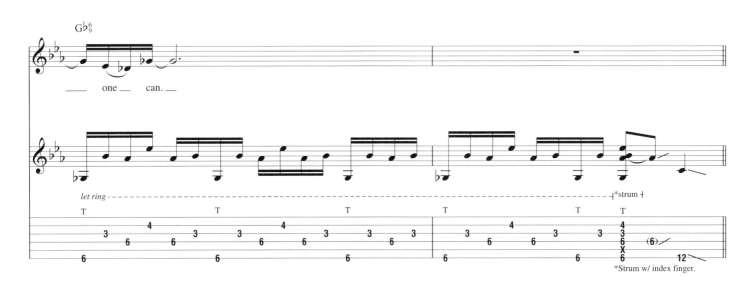

_____ one _____ can. _____

*Strum w/ index finger.

Interlude

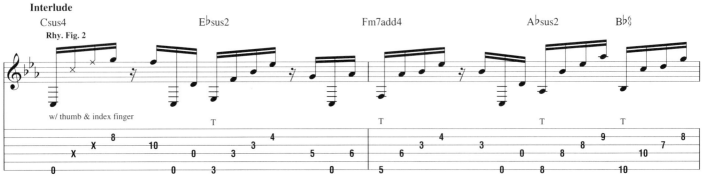

w/ thumb & index finger

2. To -

Verse
Gtr. 1: w/ Rhy. Fig. 1 (4 times)

night she's out ___ to lose ___ her - self ___ and

find a high ___ on Peach - tree Street. ___

From mixed drinks to tech - no beats ___ it's al - ways ___ heav -

- y in - to ev - 'ry - thing. ___ She comes ___

Pre-Chorus

___ and goes, ___ she comes ___ and goes ___ like no

Rhy. Fig. 3

w/ thumb & index finger

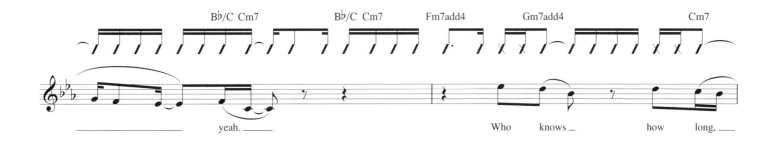

yeah. Who knows how long,

To Coda ⊕

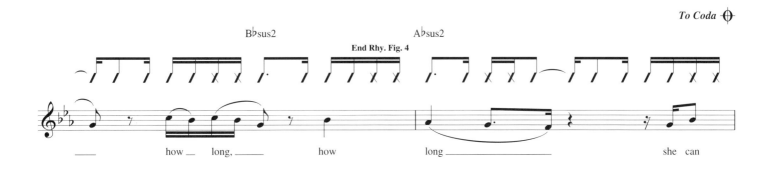

how long, how long she can

Interlude
Gtr. 1: w/ Rhy. Fig. 2

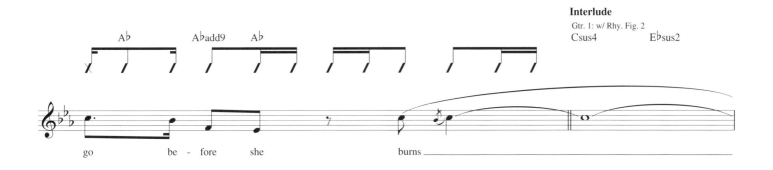

go be - fore she burns

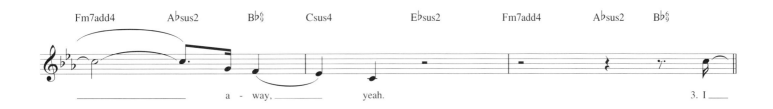

a - way, yeah. 3. I

Verse

can't be her an - gel now. You know it's

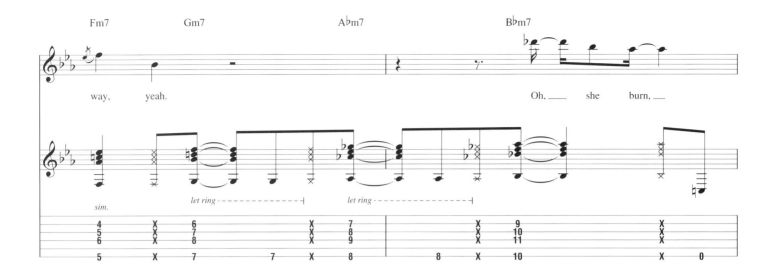

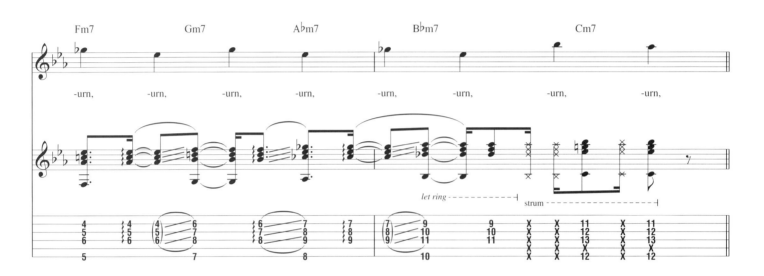

Interlude

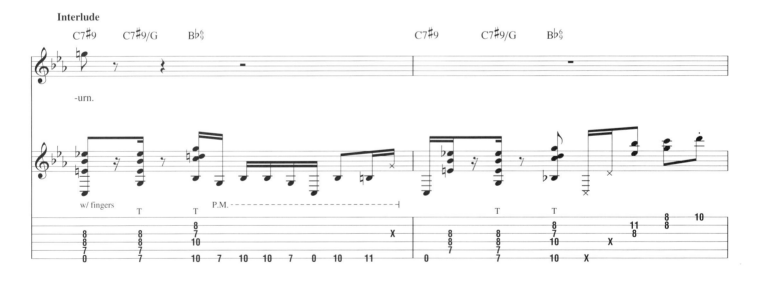

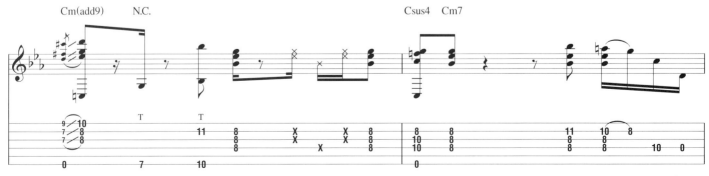

114

can, yeah, like no ___ one can. ___ She comes

___ and she goes. ___ She's sl ip -

D.S. al Coda

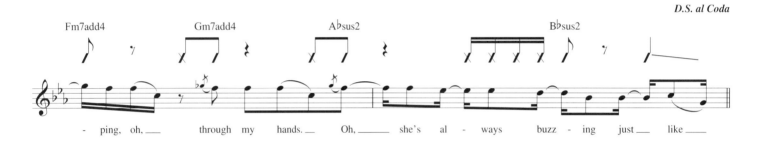

- ping, oh, ___ through my hands. ___ Oh, ___ she's al - ways buzz - ing just ___ like ___

⊕ **Coda**

Outro

Gtr. 1: w/ Rhy. Fig. 1 (2 1/2 times)

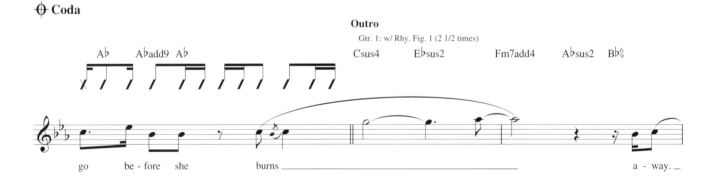

go be - fore she burns ___ a - way. ___

___ Yeah, yeah, yeah.

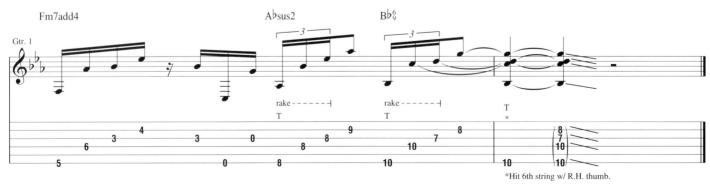

*Hit 6th string w/ R.H. thumb.

OUT OF MY MIND

Words and Music by
John Mayer

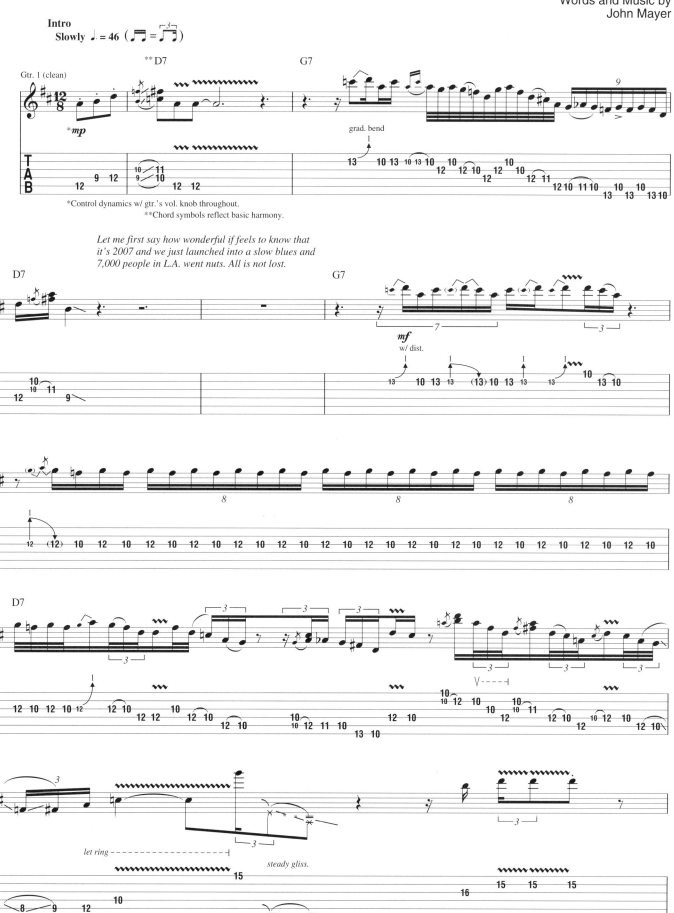

Let me first say how wonderful if feels to know that it's 2007 and we just launched into a slow blues and 7,000 people in L.A. went nuts. All is not lost.

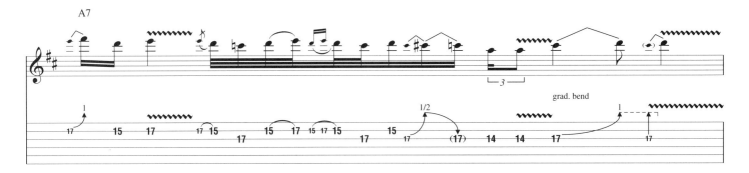

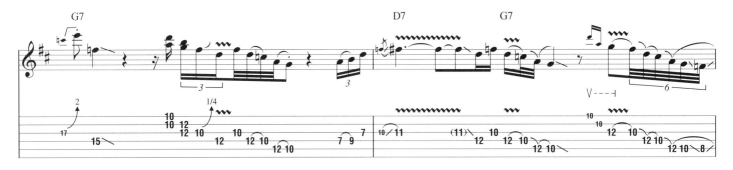

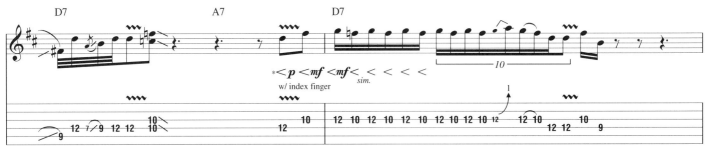

*Vol. swells. While manipulating gtr.'s vol. knob w/ pinky, pluck notes upward w/ index finger (next 8 meas.).

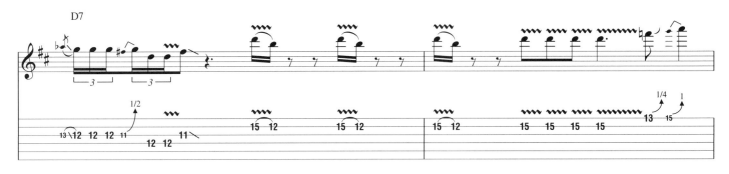

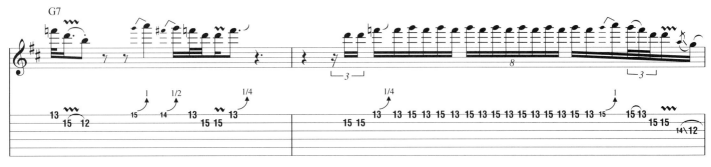

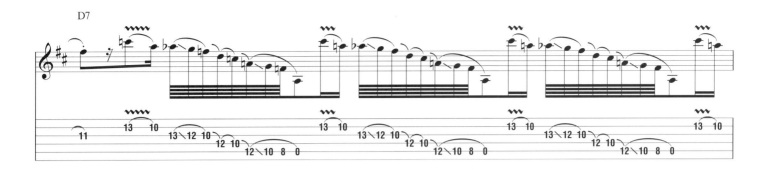

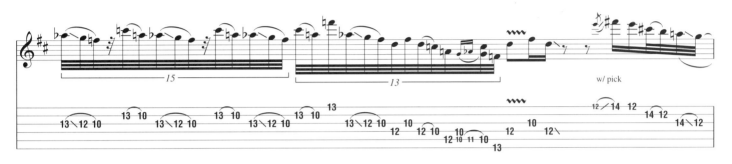

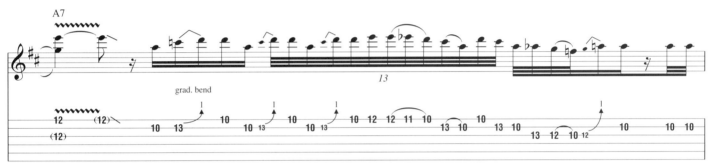

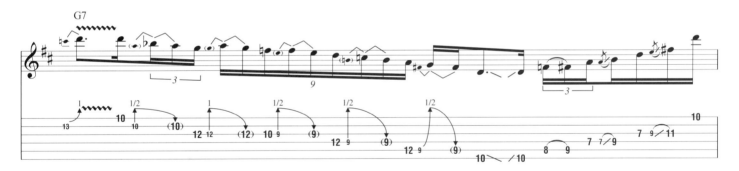

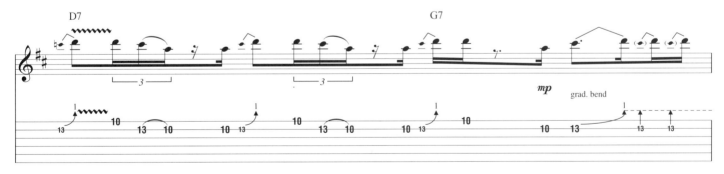

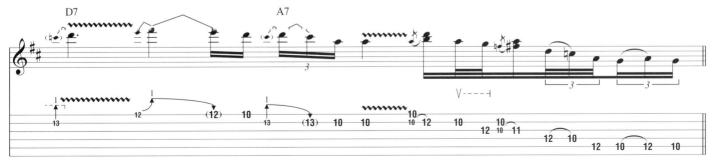

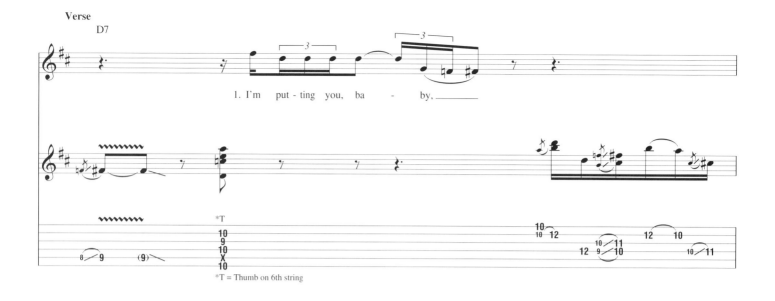

*T = Thumb on 6th string

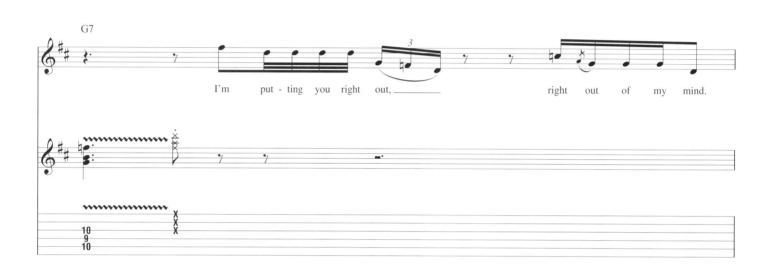

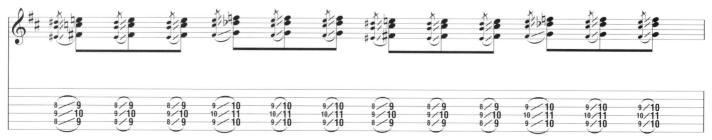

I'm put-ting you, ba-by, _____ ha, ha, ha,

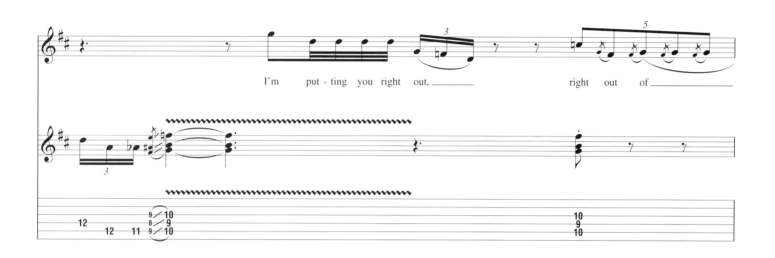

I'm put-ting you right out, _____ right out of _____

_____ my mind.

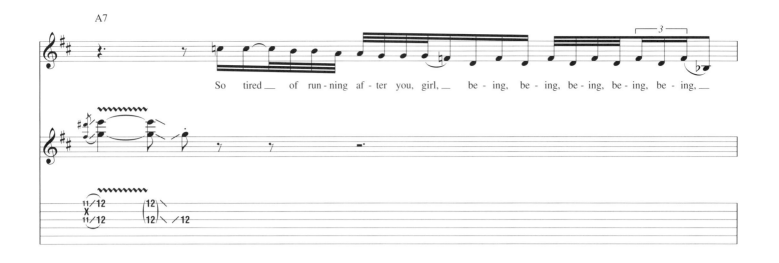

So tired__ of run-ning af-ter you, girl,__ be - ing, be - ing, be - ing, be - ing, be - ing,__

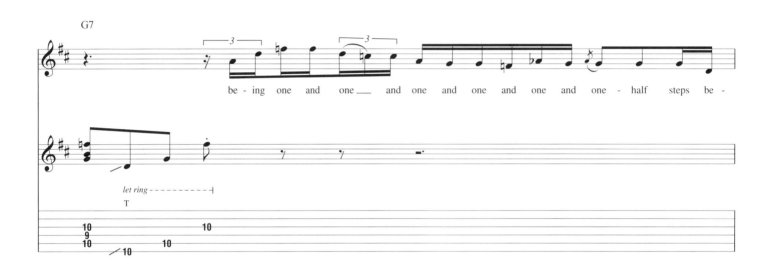

be - ing one and one__ and one and one and one and one-half steps be -

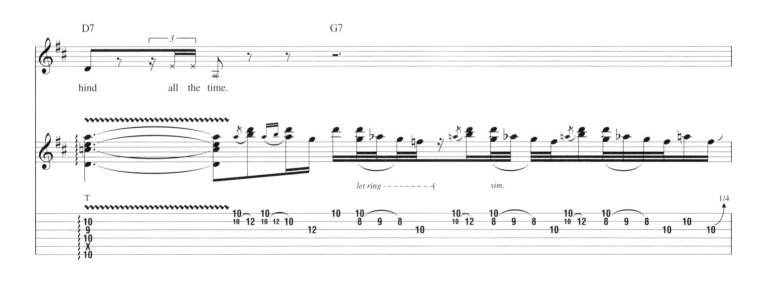

hind   all the time.

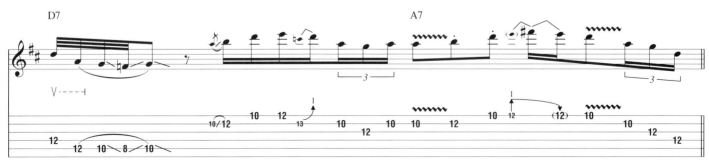

*Execute trill by sliding between notes.

*Trill normally.   **Pick strings indicated behind nut while simultaneously hammering 4th string.

124

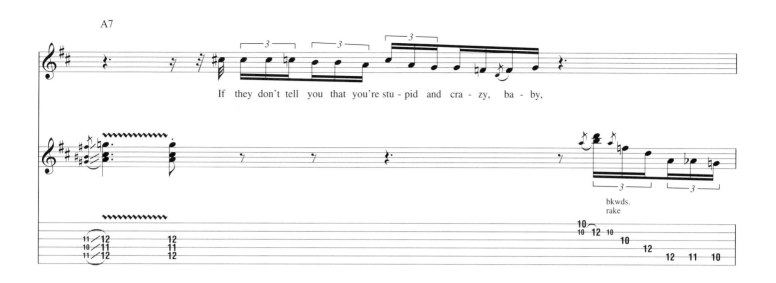

If they don't tell you that you're stu - pid and cra - zy, ba - by,

no, _____ they're just as messed up as you is.

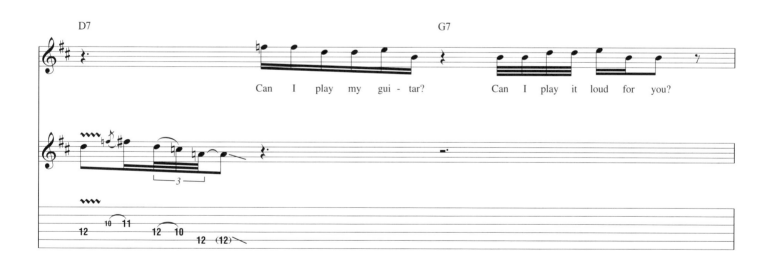

Can I play my gui - tar? Can I play it loud for you?

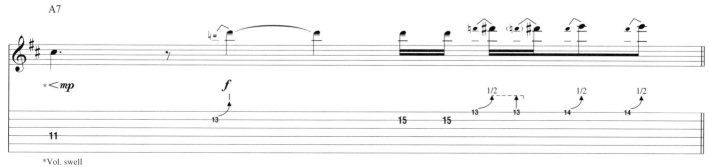

*Vol. swell

Guitar Solo

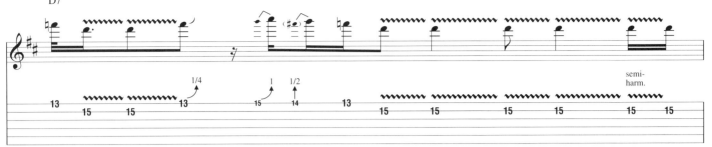

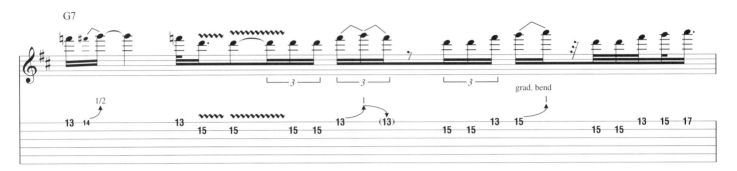

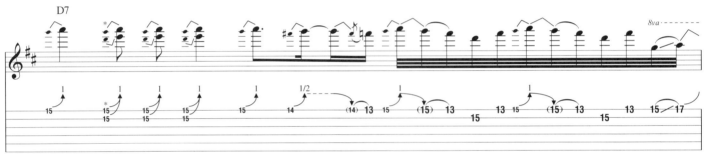

*Catch and bend both strings w/ ring finger.

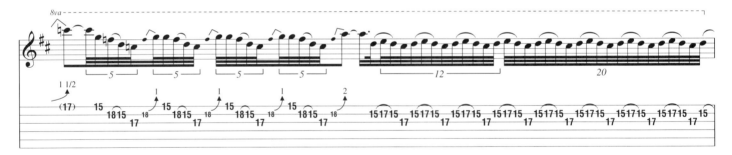

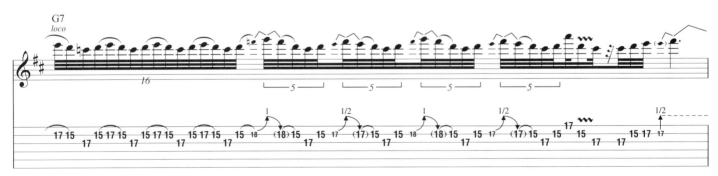

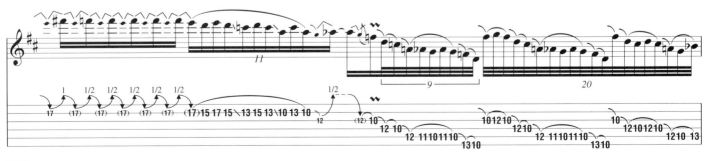

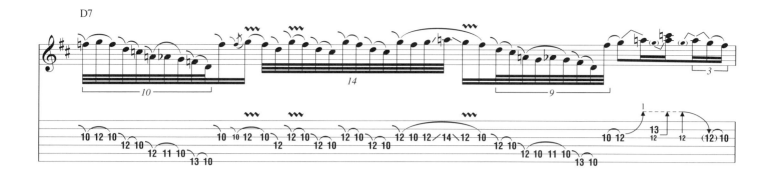

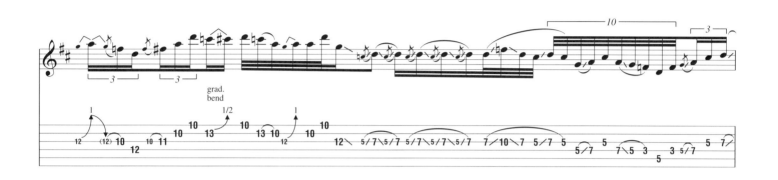

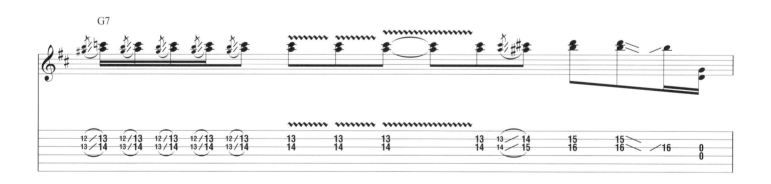

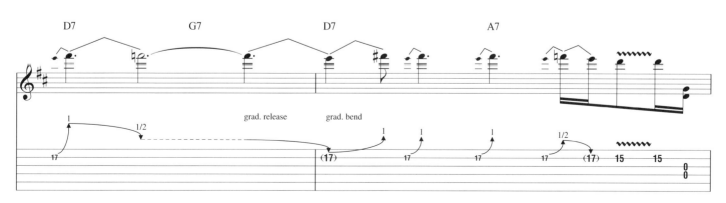

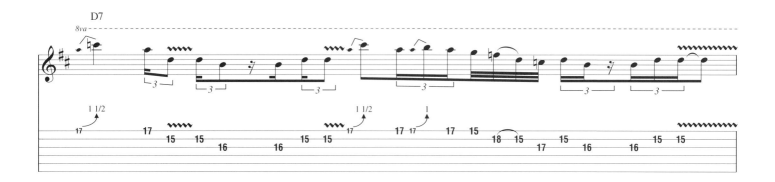

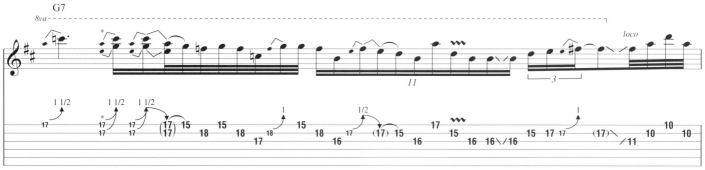

*Catch and bend both strings as before.

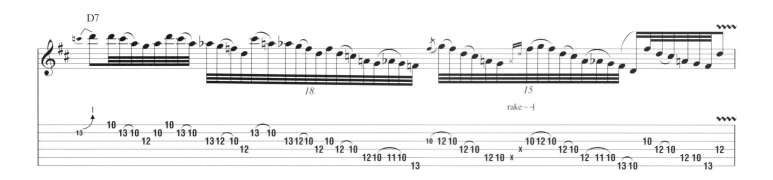

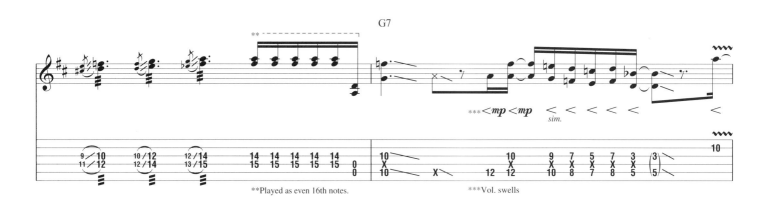

**Played as even 16th notes.

***Vol. swells

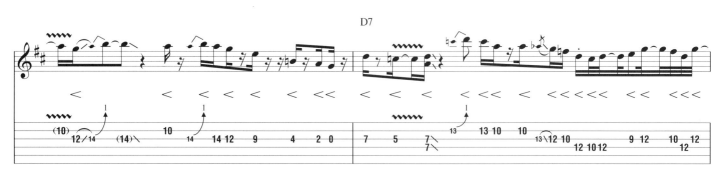

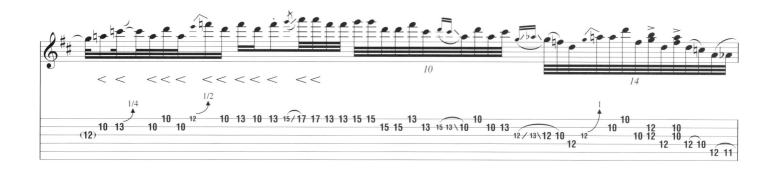

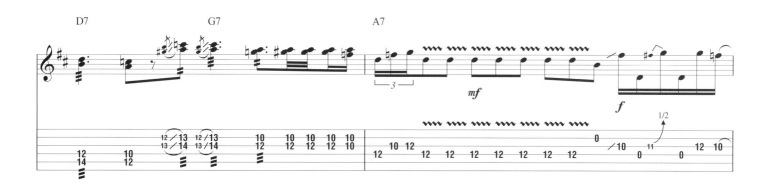

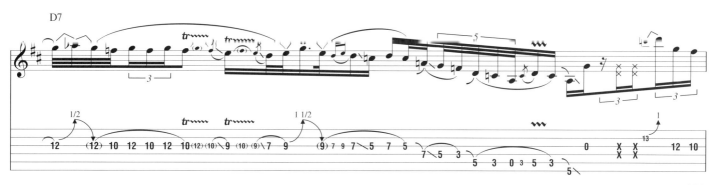

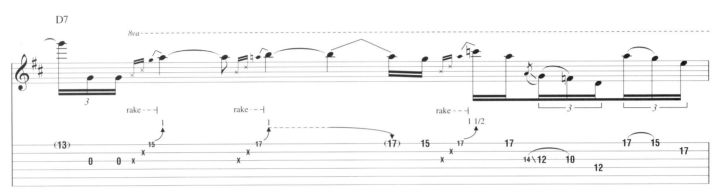

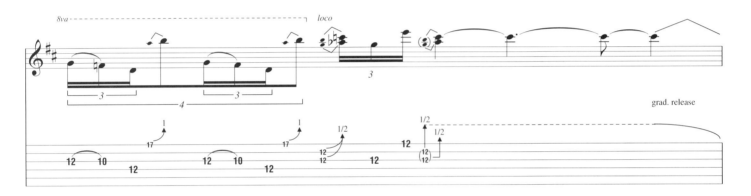

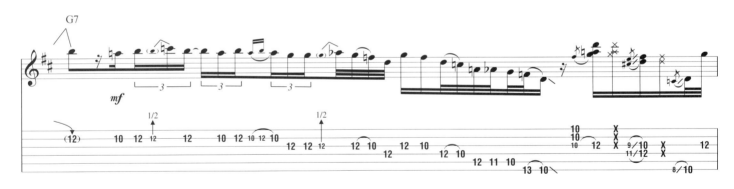

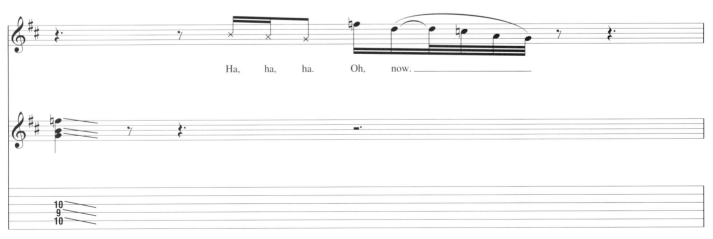

Ha, ha, ha. Oh, now. _____

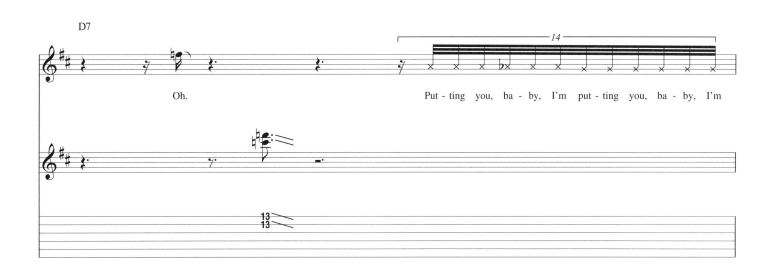

Oh.

Put - ting you, ba - by, I'm put - ting you, ba - by, I'm

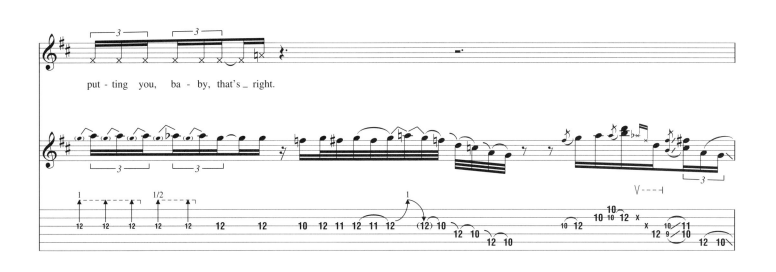

put - ting you, ba - by, that's _ right.

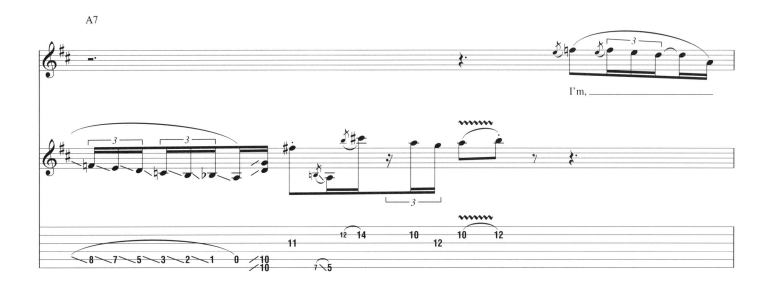

I'm, ___

I'm put - ting you, ba - by, ___ right out, right out, right

131

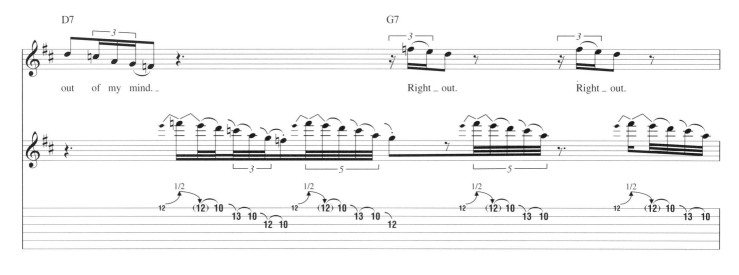

out   of my mind.___   Right _ out.   Right _ out.

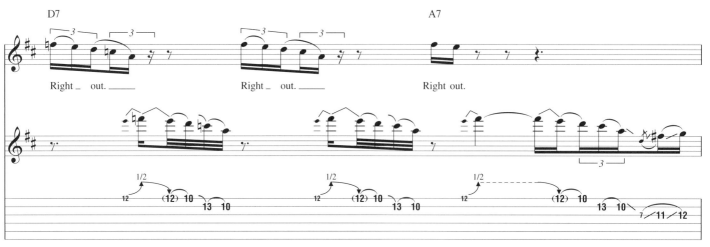

Right _ out. _____   Right _ out. _____   Right out.

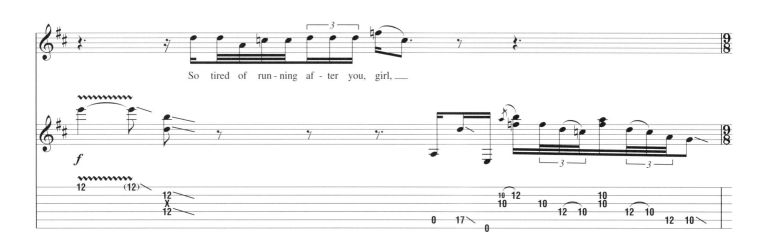

So   tired of run-ning af - ter you, girl, ___

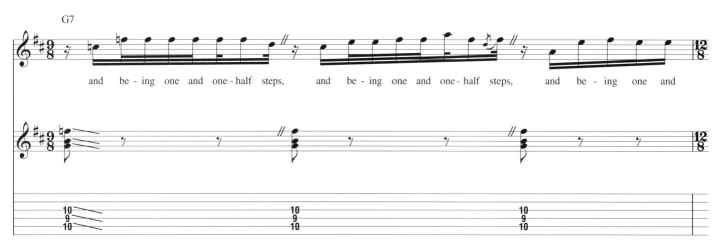

and   be - ing one and one-half steps,   and   be - ing one and one-half steps,   and   be - ing one and

A little slower, freely

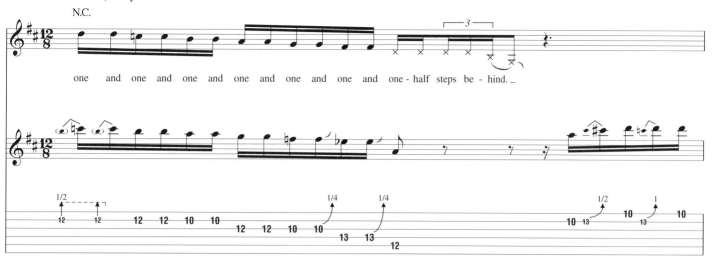

one and one and one and one and one and one and one-half steps be-hind.

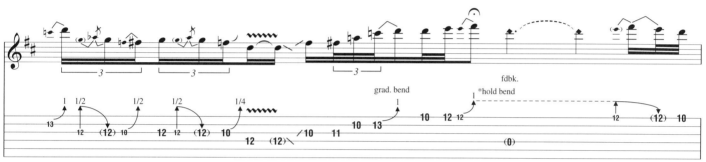

grad. bend

fdbk.

*hold bend

*Bend is held through feedback but doesn't sound.

Free time

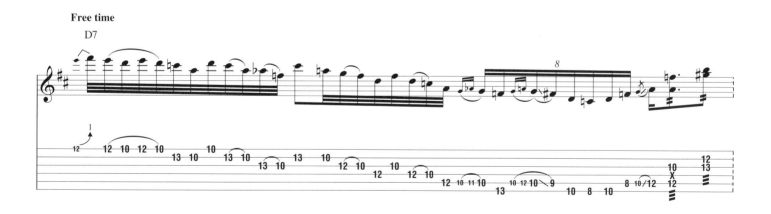

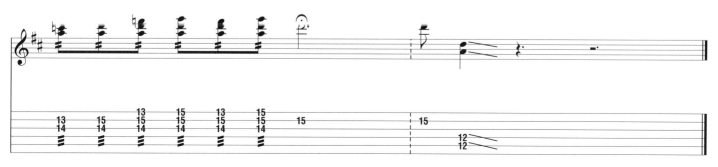

133

VULTURES

Words and Music by
John Mayer, Pino Paladino
and Steven Jordan

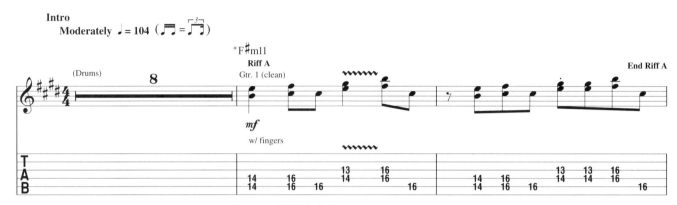

*Chord symbols reflect implied harmony.

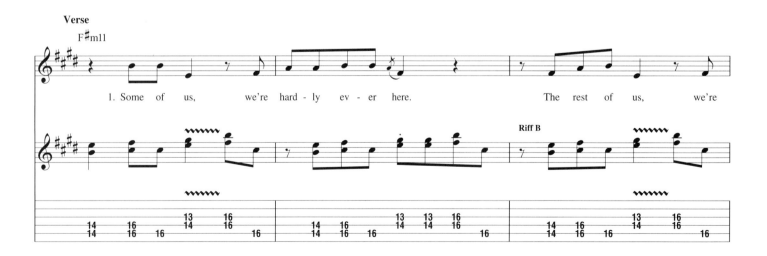

1. Some of us, we're hard-ly ev-er here. The rest of us, we're

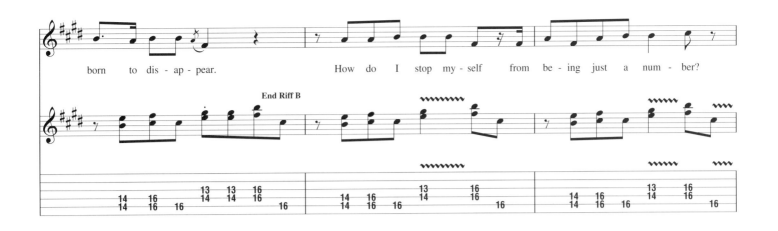

born to dis - ap - pear.   How do I stop my - self from be - ing just a num - ber?

End Riff B

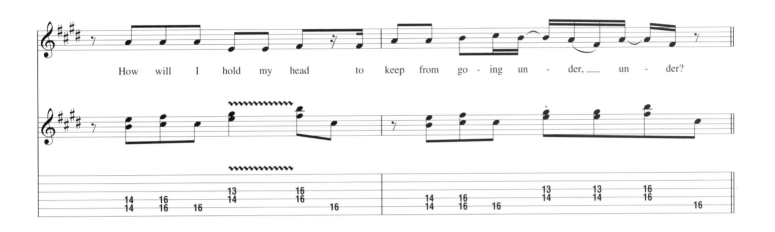

How will I hold my head to keep from go - ing un - der, ___ un - der?

% Chorus

Amaj9   B⁶₉sus4

Down to the wi - re.   I want - ed wa - ter but I'll walk through the fi - re.

Amaj9

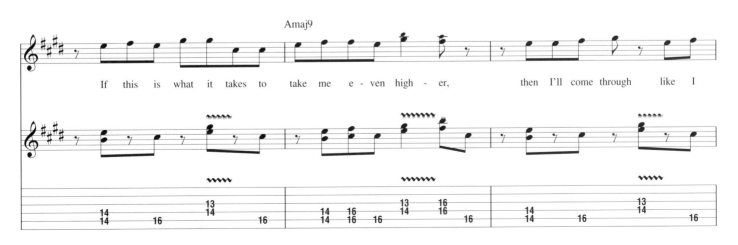

If this is what it takes to take me e - ven high - er,   then I'll come through like I

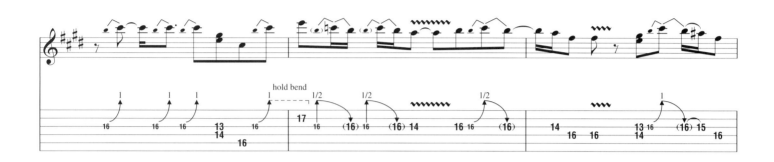

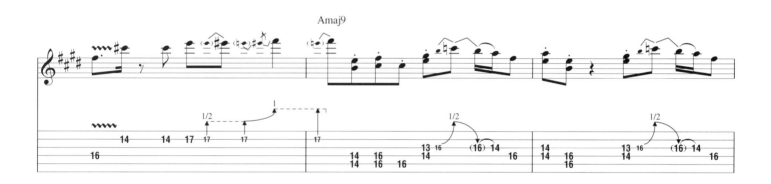

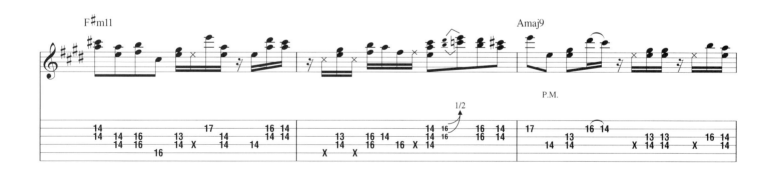

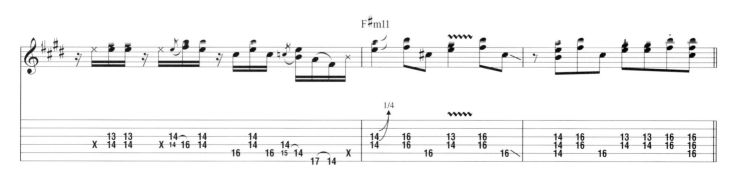

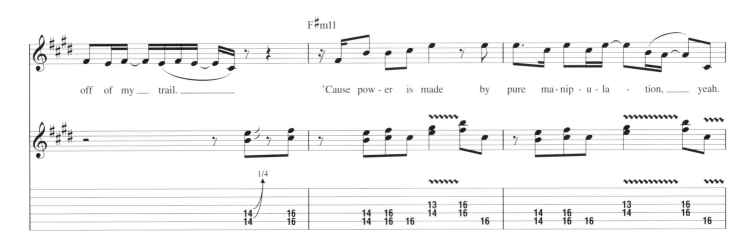

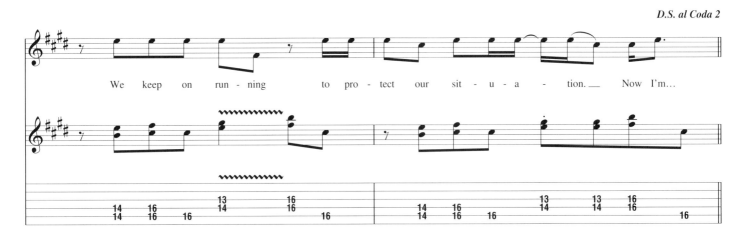

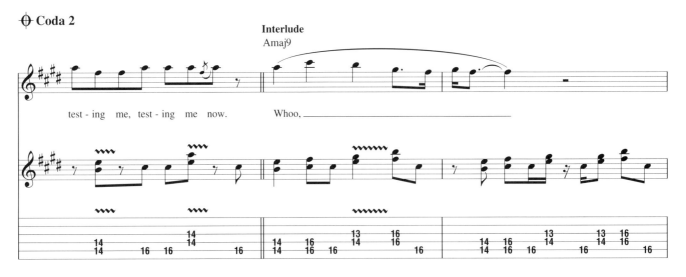

Outro

F#m11

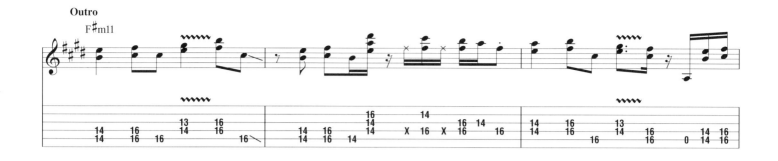

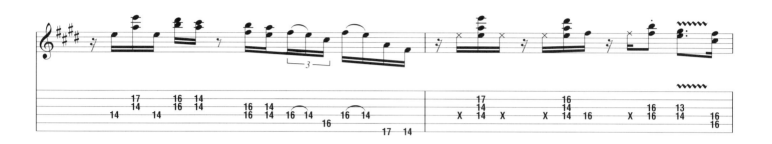

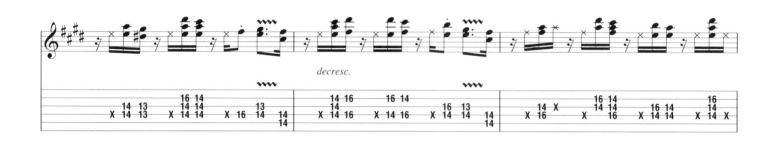

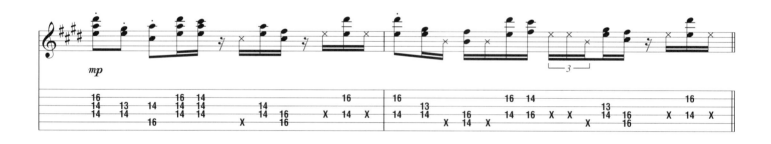

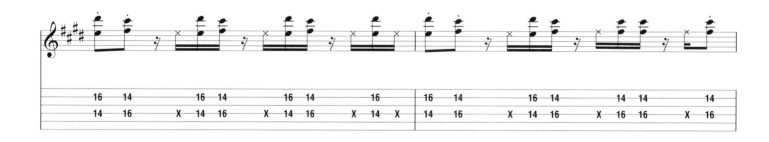

N.C.

*Played as straight 16th notes.

Free time

N.C.(F#m)

WHO DID YOU THINK I WAS

Words and Music by
John Mayer

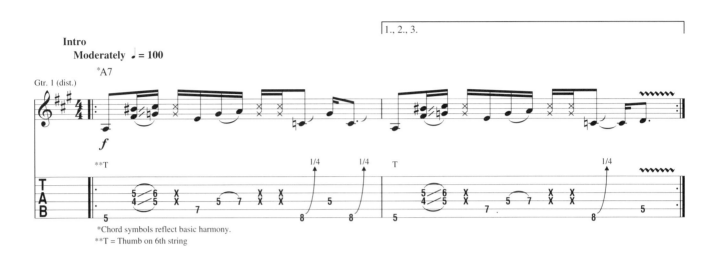

*Chord symbols reflect basic harmony.
**T = Thumb on 6th string

1. I got   half a   smile __ and   ze - ro   shame.
morn - ing   when __ the   day __   be - gins,
one who   plays __ the   qui - et   songs?

I got a re - flec - tion   with __ a   dif - f'rent __   name. __
I make   up my   mind __   but change   it   back   a - gain.
Is   he the   one __   who turns   the   la -   dies on?

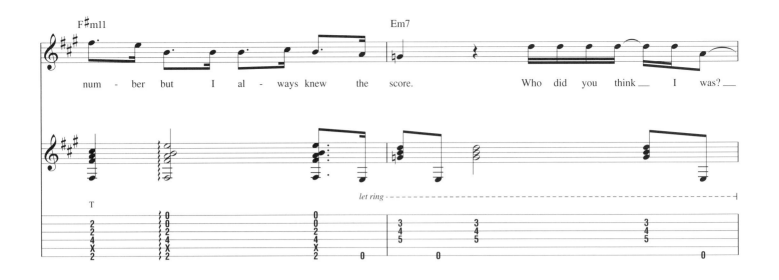

num - ber but I al - ways knew the score. Who did you think__ I was?__

To Coda ⊕

D.S. al Coda
(take 2nd ending)

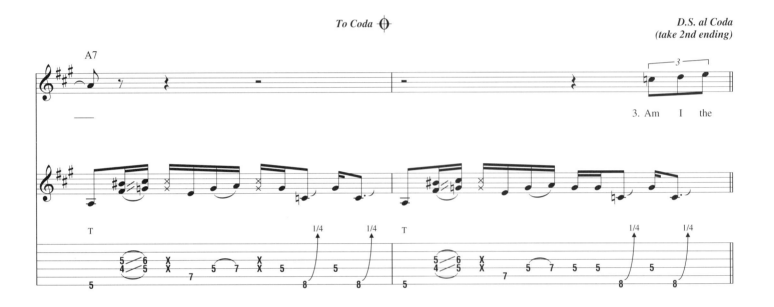

3. Am I the

⊕ **Coda**

Guitar Solo

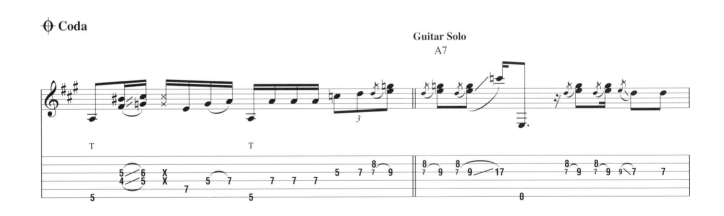

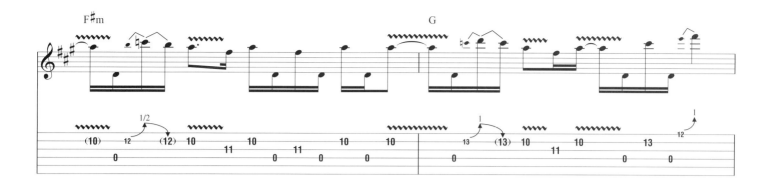

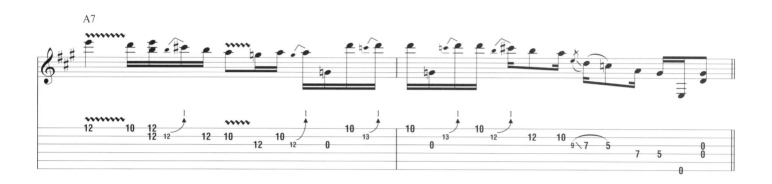

Bridge

Here is a line that you won't un-der-stand: _

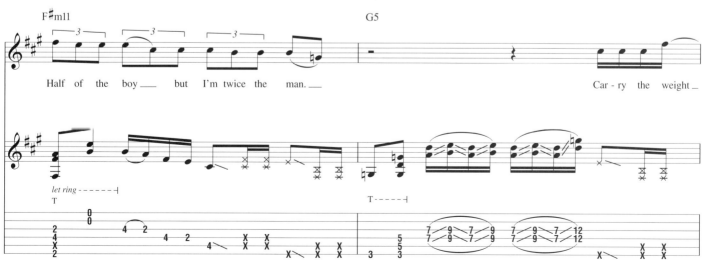

Half of the boy _ but I'm twice the man. _ Car - ry the weight _

Na na na_____ na na na. Na na na na na na na na na na.

Na na na_____ na na na. Na na na_____ na na na.

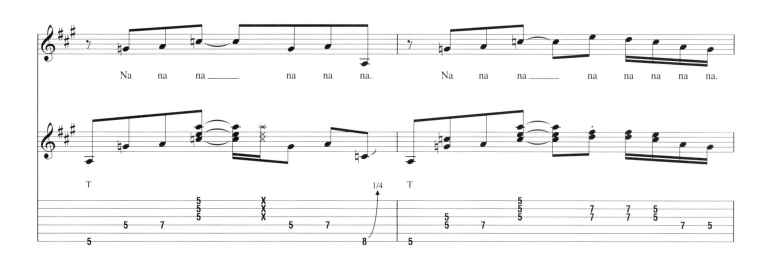

Na na na_____ na na na. Na na na_____ na na na na.

Outro-Guitar Solo

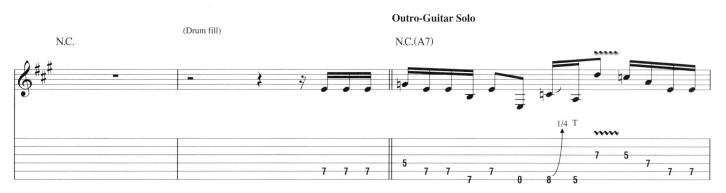

(Drum fill)

N.C.   N.C.(A7)

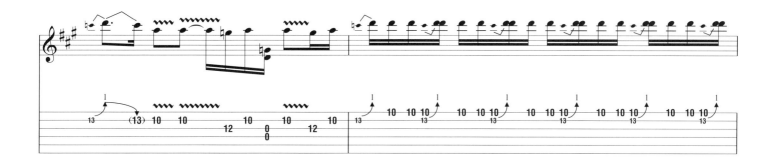

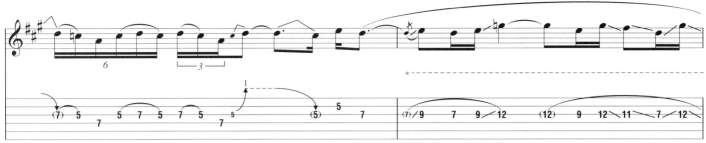

*Using a gtr. w/ Stratocaster style electronics, quickly move pickup
selector back and forth between neck and bridge positions.

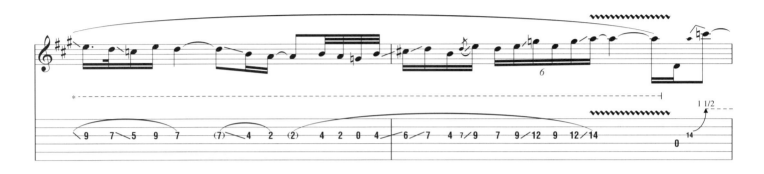

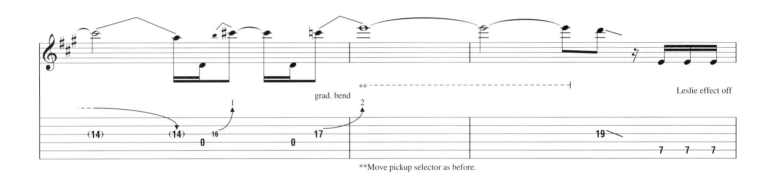

grad. bend

**Move pickup selector as before.

Leslie effect off

Na na na___ na na na na na.

WHY GEORGIA

Words and Music by
John Mayer

Gtr. 1: w/ Rhy. Fig. 1 (6 times)

yeah. Four more ex - its to

my a - part - ment, but I am tempt - ed to

Gtr. 1: w/ Rhy. Fig. 2

keep the car in drive and leave it all be -

hind. 'Cause I

(cont. in slashes)

§ **Pre-Chorus**

2nd time, Gtr. 3: w/ Rhy. Fig. 3

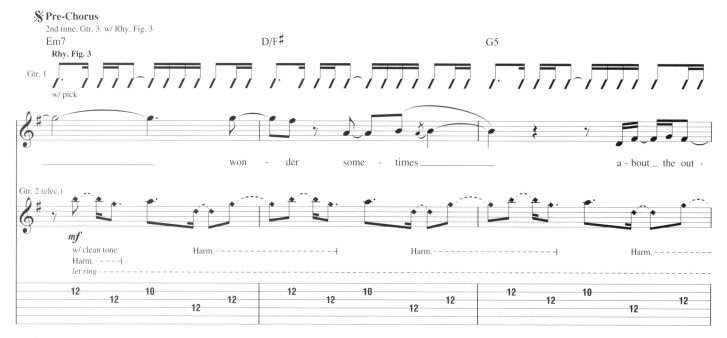

won - der some - times a - bout the out -

153

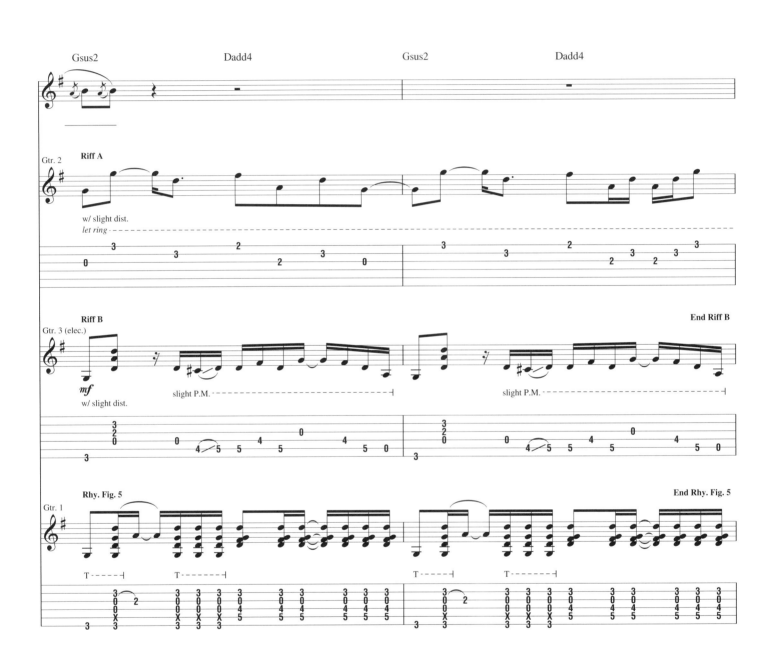

Gtr. 1: w/ Rhy. Fig. 2

C$^6_9$

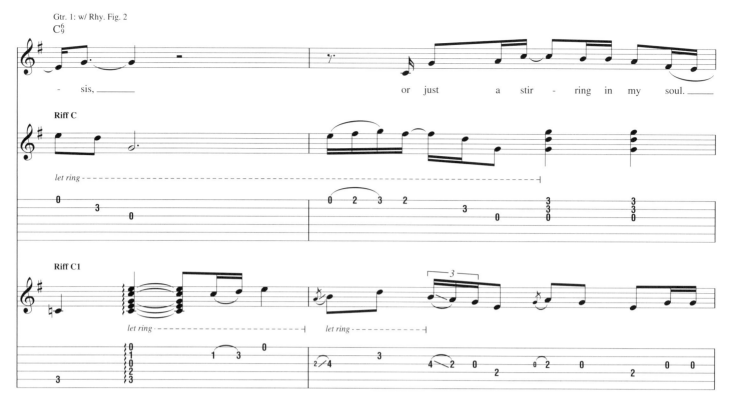

- sis, _____   or   just   a   stir - ring   in   my   soul. _____

Riff C

let ring -

Riff C1

let ring - - - - - - - - - - - - -   *let ring - - - - - - - - - - - -*

D.S. al Coda

Gtr. 1: w/ Rhy. Fig. 5

Gsus2   Dadd4   Gsus2   Dadd4

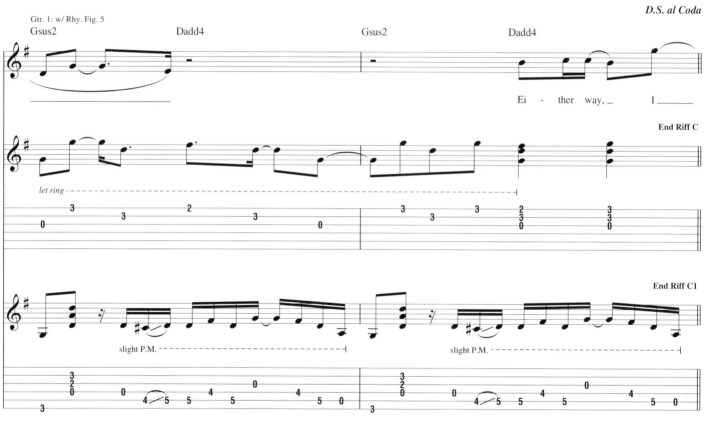

Ei - ther way, ___   I _____

End Riff C

let ring -

End Riff C1

slight P.M. -   *slight P.M. -*

🜚 **Coda**

                                                                        Bridge
                                                                        Gtrs. 2 & 3 tacet

G5   Gmaj7   G5   Fsus2   B♭sus2

Gtrs.   Gtr. 1
1, 2 & 3

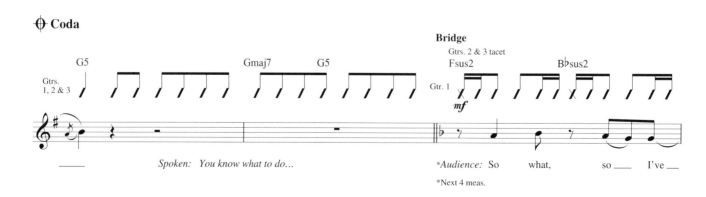

mf

_____   *Spoken: You know what to do...*   *Audience:* So   what,   so ___   I've

                                                            Next 4 meas.

156

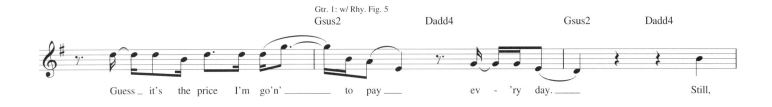

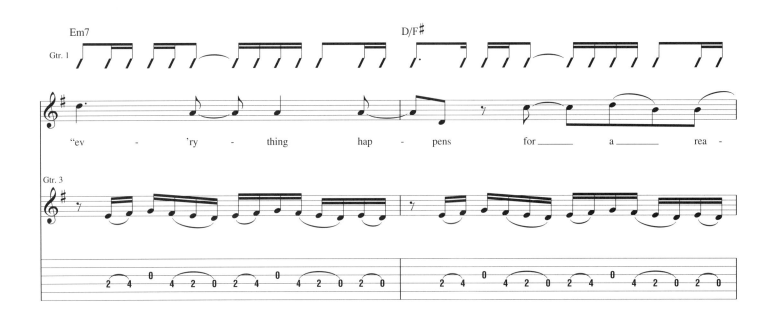

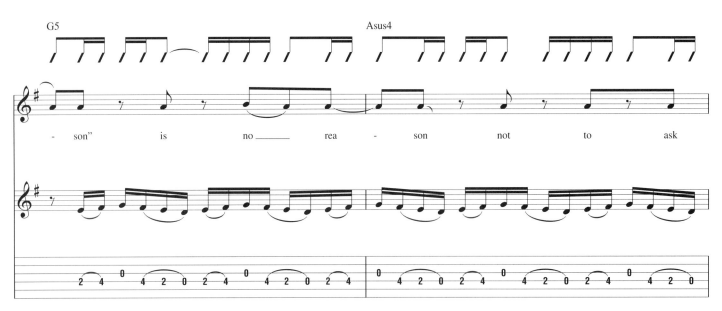

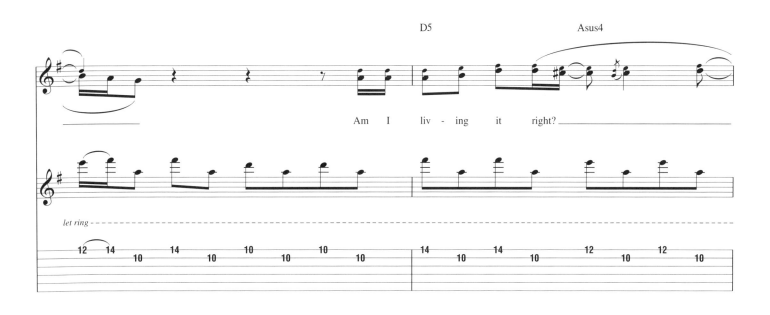

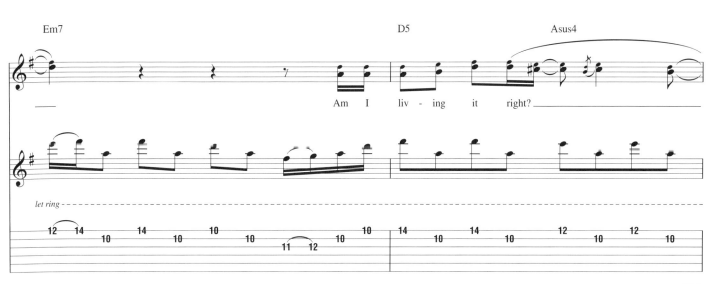

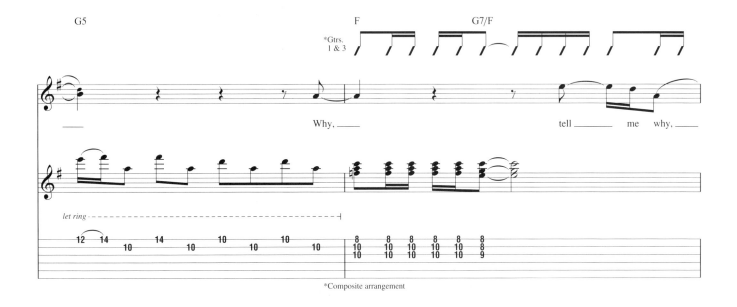

Why, _____ tell _____ me why,

*Gtrs. 1 & 3

*Composite arrangement

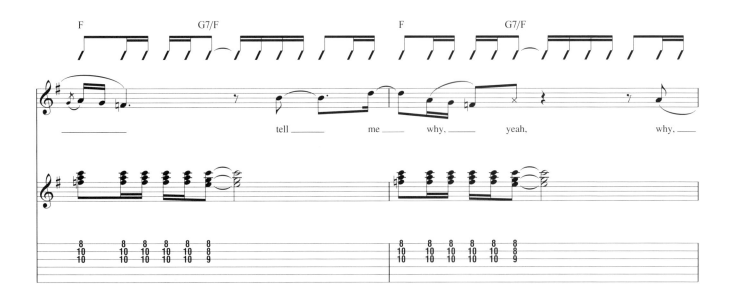

_____ tell _____ me _____ why, _____ yeah, _____ why, _____

Freely

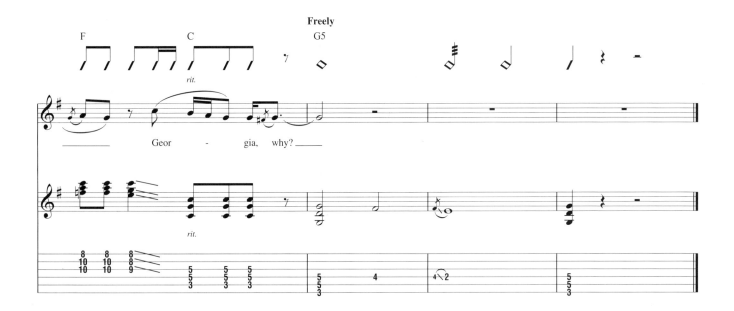

_____ Geor - gia, why? _____

rit.